Discove State

CW00879685

*Muggy days and nights, that ole Southern drawl
and a leisurely pace*

The theme of song and epic novels, loved, envied and even pitied: the Southern States. No other region of the US is considered so politically, historically, linguistically and culturally homogeneous as *the South,* a tradition and a concept familiar to all US citizens. To many it connotes muggy summer heat, the unhurried cadences of the southern drawl and traditionbound life style.

Visitors may well doubt whether this hackneyed idea of the South still applies. One invention has changed everything here: air conditioning. Without it, the Southern States would probably never have made the leap into the 20th century. Thanks to air conditioning, the South is the 'boomingest' region in the US, despite Dixieland music, plantations and the celebrated *Southern mansions,* sumptuous antebellum houses fronted by wide porches and elegant but sturdy columns. The plantation houses were the 'cas-

A gracious Southern mansion: Boon Hall Plantation in South Carolina

tles' of the great landowners of the Deep South before the War between the States, elsewhere known as the Civil War (1861-65). *Downtown,* Atlanta, Memphis and Nashville, to name three major urban centres, are spiked with skyscrapers and criss-crossed by grids of freeways, vibrantly attuned to modern living. Radios blare out pop and rock rather than country music. Agriculture has yielded to business conducted on a global scale. Of all US migrations of recent years, none is so far-reaching in its implications as the mass move to the South.

Not all that long ago – about three quarters of a century – a columnist of German descent wrote a series of essays entitled 'The Sahara of the Bozart', meaning *beaux-arts,* in snide imitation of the Southern pronunciation of French. In this dated but scorching critique of Southern culture, H.L. Mencken, a sardonic satirist and inveterate cigar smoker, condemned the South as a vast region nearly the size of Europe but intellectually and culturally as sterile as the Sahara 'worn-out

Gone with the Wind? Early morning in Atlanta

farms', 'shabby cities' and 'paralyzed cerebrums'.

Mencken's caustic comments enraged Southerners. They set to work to discredit his statements. Mencken enjoyed the inadvertently comical rebuttals of his rebarbative wit so much that he published excerpts from letters in a second printing of his essay. They are an excellent source of information on what cultural achievements were particularly prized by Southerners at the time.

Who has not heard of Asa G. Candler, runs one wrathful comment, whose name is synonymous with Coca-Cola, a Georgia product?

The first Sunday-school in the world, contributed another, was opened in Savannah. And so on and so on.

Mencken hit the nail on the head when he described the Southern narrow-mindedness and suspicion of Northerners still felt in 1916, 73 years after the Civil War: A casual word, and the united press of the South will be upon your trail, denouncing you bitterly as a scoundrelly damn yankee, a 'Bolshevik Jew'.

You'll still see the Dixie flag with its bold St Andrew's cross and eleven stars for the states that seceded from the Union in 1860/61 proudly flown in many a Southern town and waved at parades. In Georgia some members of the state legislature even wanted to see the Confederate flag flown throughout the country on a footing of symbolic equality with the star-spangled banner of the United States.

However, many of the negative connotations of slavery and oppression for which the Confederate flag once stood, have vanished. The eleven Southern States now represent a global outlook. From Atlanta, Georgia, CNN reaches out to the world with its communications network, giving meaning to the buzzword of the Global Village. Its directors and policy-makers regard nationalism, regionalism or any sort of parochialism as an infringement of the CNN code. Rockets, the ultimate in

MARCO ⊕ POLO
USA • SOUTHERN STATES
NEW ORLEANS

with Local Tips

The author's special recommendations are
highlighted in yellow throughout this guide

There are five symbols to help you find your way around this guide:

Marco Polo's top recommendations – the best in each category

sites with a scenic view

places where the local people meet

places where young people get together

(100/A1)

pages and coordinates for the Road Atlas of the Southern States
(U/A1) *coordinates for the City Map of New Orleans inside back cover*

MARCO ⊕ POLO

Travel guides and language guides in this series:

Alaska • Algarve • Amsterdam • Australia/Sydney • Bahamas • Barbados
Berlin • Brittany • California • Canada • Channel Islands • Costa
Brava/Barcelona • Costa del Sol/Granada • Côte d'Azur • Crete • Cuba
Cyprus • Dominican Republic • Eastern Canada • Eastern USA • Florence
Florida • Gran Canaria • Greek Islands/Aegean • Ibiza/Formentera • Ireland
Istanbul • Lanzarote • London • Mallorca • Malta • Mexico • New York
New Zealand • Normandy • Paris • Prague • Rhodes • Rome • San Francisco
Scotland • South Africa • Southwestern USA • Tenerife • Turkish Coast
Tuscany • USA: Southern States • Venice • Western Canada

French • German • Italian • Spanish

*Marco Polo would be very interested to hear your
comments and suggestions. Please write to:*

North America:
Marco Polo North America
70 Bloor Street East
Oshawa, Ontario, Canada
(B) 905-436-2525

United Kingdom:
GeoCenter International Ltd
The Viables Centre
Harrow Way
Basingstoke, Hants RG22 4BJ

Cover photograph: Saxophone man in New Orleans on the Mississippi (Mauritius AGE)
*Photos: Focus: Gould Matrix (24); Lade: Behnke (71), Proctor (64); Layda (4, 6, 55);
Mauritius: GFP (36), Hubatka (99), Lindner (32), Noble (53), Schmied (78), Vidler (50, 72, 88);
Schapowalow: China Photo (81), Novak (38, 82); Schuster: Bull (9, 22, 44), Kummels (12, 87), Layda (28),
Rangow (77), Schmied (62), Tauqueur (18); Transglobe: Braasch (59), Granitsas (15), Taylor (42)*

1st edition 2000
© Mairs Geographischer Verlag, Ostfildern, Germany
Author: Michael Schwelien
Translator: Joan Clough
English edition 2000: Gaia Text
Editorial director: Ferdinand Ranft
Chief editor: Marion Zorn
Cartography for the Road Atlas: © MapMedia Corporation, Canada; Mairs Geographischer Verlag
Design and layout: Thienhaus/Wippermann
Printed in Germany

CONTENTS

high-tech, are launched into space from Cape Canaveral, Florida. Miami and New Orleans are really cosmopolitan, not merely because they attract so many visitors from abroad. The majority of these two Southern cities' residents was born outside the US, primarily in the Caribbean basin and Central America. Bill Clinton, US president for two terms and a native of Little Rock, Arkansas, is a true liberal, willing to tolerate homosexuals in the armed forces and committed to the advancement of minorities and women in public life. His highly educated wife Hillary, a Middle-Westerner, was the first politically active First Lady since Eleanor Roosevelt.

Something very positive has always been associated with the South: *Southern hospitality.* It goes back a long way to an era when families lived far apart from each other on plantations so they depended on hospitality. This fine tradition of *Southern hospitality* has survived the test of time. Even visitors who only stay for a short time invariably notice it. Whether you're in a restaurant, are introduced to someone, you'll be enchanted with the laid-back friendliness of the Southern *drawl,* which in places like Virginia and West Virginia, can even sound like Elizabethan English played at the wrong speed: *Hi, how'y'all?,* instead of the terse Hi occasionally barked out by laconic Yankees. Southern speech sounds friendly and usually cheerful. It makes you feel that way, too. In rural areas and small towns, far from the bustle of the big cities, South-erners are genuinely interested in visitors and like chatting with them. English visitors may remember that there was sympathy in Britain for the Confederacy during the Civil War.

The southeastern seaboard was settled by English colonists in the 17th century. English colonists tried to settle at Roanoke Island off North Carolina in 1585. Jamestown, Virginia, was founded in 1607, but English colonies did not take hold in the Old Dominion until the mid-17th century. The Carolinas and Georgia were not granted a royal charter until 1663. A colony was founded in Maryland in 1634 by Cecilius Calvert, second Baron Baltimore. The Old South did not attract settlers from continental Europe in the 17th and 18th centuries except for some French Huguenots. Perhaps due to the climate, cities have never been big in the South. Long, hot, humid summers and an extended rainy season made establishing plantations an unhealthy occupation. Without the vicious institution of *slavery,* which entailed regarding *human beings* as goods and chattels, the South could never have been settled.

With an economy based on slave labour, the South was an agrarian society and had little industrial manufacturing. Tobacco was planted from the early 17th century and cotton fields, the symbol of the South, covered Mississippi and Georgia. *Those cotton fields back home,* the refrain of an old slave song sung on plantations shows that, hard as their lives were, slaves came to identify with the land they worked.

The adjective *'cotton-pickin'* is still used in the vernacular as a derogatory term connoting 'poor white trash' and what is regarded as behaviour typical of the impoverished white lower class which grew up in rural areas after the Civil War. The fledgling Republican party elected Abraham Lincoln, an opponent of slavery, 16th President of the US, in November 1860. Between December 1860 and May 1861 the following Southern States seceded from the Union: Virginia, North and South Carolina, Georgia, Florida, Alabama, Tennessee, Mississippi, Louisiana, Arkansas and Texas (this last state is not covered in the present guide). Kentucky was the sole Southern state to remain outside the Confederacy. In April 1861 hostilities between North and South broke out, the only major war ever fought in the US after 1779. At first the brilliant Virginian general, Robert E. Lee, was successful against the Yankees. The North, however, was industrialized and could put much larger armies in the field. In 1862 President Lincoln declared slavery abolished in the Confederate States. Richmond, the capital of the Confederacy, fell in 1865. During the entire war, Union armies continued to burn and plunder throughout the South, destroying cities and plantations. This is why so little is left of the fine *antebellum,* that is, pre-Civil War, architecture. The assassination of Lincoln on 14 April 1865 put an end to all policies of reconciliation. His inept successor, Andrew Johnson, refused to endorse the more radical Congressional bills initiated to aid former slaves. Called 'Reconstruction', the post-war era saw the emergence of the notorious *carpetbaggers.* The *carpetbaggers* were Yankee small businessmen and wheeler-dealers who hurried down South to make quick profits, clutching the clumsy luggage piece sewn together from carpet after which this species of racketeer is aptly named. In 1868, the former slaves were granted suffrage, the right to vote, against the will of Southern state legislatures, which refused to pass the Fourteenth Amendment to the US Constitution granting full civil rights to Negroes.

The *carpetbaggers* were not interested in rebuilding the South. Nor were Southern legislatures desirous of redressing the political and social wrongs done to African-Americans. Until the 1960s blacks had to sit in the back seats on buses. Restaurants and lavatories were segregated and blacks attended separate schools. Blacks literally lived *on the other side of the railroad tracks –* in the worst part of town. President John F. Kennedy initiated the legislative process which guaranteed all races equality before the law. His successor, Lyndon B. Johnson, endeavored to complete the process. The Reverend Martin Luther King, who, like both Kennedys, was assassinated, was the leader of the Civil Rights Movement. Idealistic young Northerners who went South in the cause of Civil Rights were known as *Freedom Riders.*

The Southern States are not nearly as culturally and economically homogeneous as one might think. If you start your trip through the South in northern Virginia outside Washington, D.C., the nation's capital, and go south as far as New Orleans, the capital of jazz, taking several detours to explore the regions you pass through on the way, you'll have covered an area about as large as Western Europe.

The Washington *suburbs,* the outlying fringes of the hub of power, extend far into northern Virginia. The influence exerted by the capital does not end there. Many of the lush Virginia farms with white-fenced paddocks for sleek saddle horses and small white clapboard houses surrounded by fallow fields are the weekend retreats of commuters who work in Washington, D.C. Much of the Eastern Shore of Virginia between the Chesapeake Bay and the Atlantic and the Carolinas are outside the Washington catchment area. Mass tourism from abroad has not yet caught on here and probably will not for some time to come. Canadians, however, have discovered the island beaches and fragrant pine barrens of Assateague and Chincoteague in Maryland and northern Virginia. English Sunday Supplement writers gush about beautiful Charleston, South Carolina. The barrier islands of the North Carolina Outer Banks, where the northern Labrador Current meets the Gulf Stream, boast long, lonely beaches with sands that shift at every storm. They have remained virtually untouched since Orville and Wilbur Wright launched their first successful attempts at manned flight in North Carolina. What has changed beyond recognition is the high-tech *Research Triangle,* the North Carolina cities of Durham, Raleigh and Charlotte, one of several Silicon Valley clones. Here a far-sighted regional policy has promoted high-tech growth industries and university collaboration in research and development.

The Appalachian mountain chain runs through the northernmost Southern States. Stretching for 2,600 km from

A different South: the palm beach at Fort Lauderdale

History at a glance

35 000 years ago
Indians migrate across the Bering Strait to Alaska, eventually reaching Florida

1492
Christopher Columbus reaches the New World but thinks he is in India, hence the name Indians

17th century
Five colonies are founded by royal charter on the eastern seaboard, with the first successful Southern settlement, Jamestown (1607), followed by Williamsburg (1632). The British Crown also grants proprietary colonies to important individuals like Cecilius Calvert

4.7.1776
Declaration of Independence: Drawn up by John Adams, Benjamin Franklin and Thomas Jefferson, the Declaration of Independence marked the colonies' break with Great Britain

1775–1783
The War of Independence. Hostilities commenced before the Declaration of Independence

21.11.1789
The Constitution is ratified by North Carolina, the last Southern state to do so

1789–1797
George Washington 1st President of the United States. Kentucky (1792) and Tennessee (1796) join the Union

1803
Louisiana is purchased by the US for 15 million dollars from Napoleon I

1819
Florida is purchased from Spain

1861–1865
Civil War: The North becomes increasingly industrialized while the Southern economy is agrarian and slave-based. Abraham Lincoln, an opponent of slavery, is elected president. Eleven Southern States secede from the Union

22.11.1963
President John F. Kennedy is shot in Dallas, Texas. His successor, Lyndon B. Johnson, signs into law the Kennedy policies of integration and racial equality

1994
Republican majorities in both houses of Congress. The South votes almost entirely Republican

Summer 1996
The summer Olympics in Atlanta are attended by 3 million visitors

1999
Candidates for the presidential election in 2000 are from the South: Elizabeth Dole from South Carolina, George Bush, Governor of Texas, Vice-President Al Gore from Tennessee

the St. Lawrence River to Georgia, its ridges rise to elevations of 1,500 to 2,000 m. The scenery of West Virginia, Kentucky and Tennessee is moulded by the Appalachians. The term Appalachia often refers to the West Virginia mining valleys, which have remained nearly as poor as they were when Walker Evans photographed their impoverished inhabitants during the Roosevelt era. Kentucky is the Blue Grass state, famous for rolling hills and horse breeding. Further to the west the land flattens out. The turgid brown waters of the mighty Mississippi roll past Memphis, the capital of Rock 'n' Roll, where Elvis was discovered. Across the river is Arkansas, one of the poorest states in the South, with an agrarian economy. Bill Clinton and Senator Fulbright are its famous sons.

Louisiana, Mississippi and Alabama are known as the *Deep South*. Summers here are indescribably hot and humid. In the course of mass migrations from the rapidly deindustrialising North to other parts of the South, UNESCO became aware of the discrepancies in living standards within the world's richest nation. In fact, some rural sections of the Deep South can only be described as Third World, with many people living at a subsistence level otherwise encountered only in parts of Africa and South America. In some areas of Mississippi, small farmers still count themselves fortunate when they are given mules to plough their fields. Louisiana is the world's largest producer and exporter of rice yet even the agricultural sector has failed to create as many jobs as might be expected. The bayou country is ideal for this usually labour-intensive crop, which, however, is here planted and harvested largely by mechanical means.

Georgia, the Peachtree State, is home to defence industries. Like Tennessee and South Carolina, where Ford, General Motors, Nissan and BMW (in Spartanburg) make cars, Georgia definitely unites extremes of poverty and affluence. Green-fields are given over to modern plants and the agriculture is declining around them. Lovely Cobb County, extending from Atlanta to the mountains, is one of the richest residential areas in the US. Atlanta, the capital of Georgia, was the 1996 venue of the Olympic Games. The modern city replacing the one described by Margaret Mitchell in the popular novel 'Gone with the Wind' is perhaps the only metropolis in the South. Participants in, and visitors to, the Olympics were surprised to find that everything in Atlanta – shopping passages, plazas and even balconies – seemed to be hidden from view or facing inward.

Florida doesn't really seem like the South even though it's the southernmost tip of the US. It has become a magnet for tourists from across the world. The fabulous beaches, luxury hotels and Art Déco residential sections of Miami are cosmopolitan. Disney World fascinates visitors from abroad as much as Americans. Crime is rife in Miami and not just in 'Miami Vice'. This is definitely not the leisurely Old South of legend and colonial tradition.

From ABC to Literature

Tips on how to understand the South

ABC

Well, alcohol is a touchy issue in parts of the South. Drink is officially frowned on in devout Southern Baptist communities. Nevertheless, you certainly can't call the South dry. Where, then, do you find the booze – beer, wine and spirits ('hard liquor' in the South) – in the land of the mint julep, Planter's Punch, Jack Daniels and Southern Comfort? You have to go to what is euphemistically termed a *package store* or an *ABC store,* – for **A**lcoholic **B**everage **C**ontrol Store. Only rarely do people come right out and call this institution what it usually is in the US: a *liquor store.* Don't be put off by the word control. Prices are often so low that devotees of strong drink will find themselves grabbing a half-gallon bottle instead of the classic *fifth,* or fifth gallon (about 0.7 l.) Low taxes are the reason the booze is so cheap down here, or at least the down-home, brewed and distilled variety. The battle has raged for years on whether *sin taxes* should be levied. Most Southern States are reluctant to go that far so you'll be able to

St. Louis Roman Catholic Cathedral, New Orleans

stock up in ABC stores for prices that will lead you into temptation.

Bible Belt

The name is apt, especially in the rural Deep South: *Bible Belt.* Entire communities attend church every Sunday. Children go to Sunday school and church socials are fun for young and old: picnics, barbecues and dances put on by churches of all denominations. Visitors are welcome too. Some denominations, including some but not all Southern Baptists, adhere strictly to the teachings of the Old Testament and almost seem to ignore the New. The upshot of so much fundamentalist piety has been legislation in some Southern States requiring state schools to give *Creationist Theory* equal weight in the curriculum with Darwin's theory of evolution. Creationist Theory takes the creation of the world as described in Genesis literally. The outcome of the court battle fought in Dayton, Tennessee, in 1925, against a schoolmaster who taught Darwinist theory, the celebrated *monkey trial,* has in practice been reversed. Itinerant preachers, another fascinating aspect of rural Deep South piety, have yielded to eloquent televangelists. Under the aegis of the powerful, all-white

Christian Coalition, fundamentalist Christianity funds the campaigns of conservative members of Congress at grassroots level. Even harmless publications are targeted by zealots. In small-town drugstores *Playboy* is on sale antiseptically sealed in plastic with the cover girl covered up. A majority in the Deep South upholds the death penalty.

Front porch

Most houses in the South are clapboard, built of wood, and painted white or in pastel colours. The salient architectural feature of Southern houses built after the late-18th century is the *front porch.* Some houses have side and back porches, two-storey verandas or single-storey porches encircling the entire structure. On hot evening the porch replaces the living room. In small towns the front porch becomes an extension of the living room. TV soap operas blare through screened, open windows while mother irons. Children loll on upholstered *swings* suspended from the porch roof. *Front porches* are an integral part of sales space in small town shops. Men sit on them, their jaws slowly moving in unison because they have a *chaw,* a wad of chewing tobacco, in their mouths. Every so often someone emits a stream of tobacco juice over the porch railing.

Country music

The states of West Virginia, Kentucky and Tennessee are home to what used to be known disparagingly as *hillbilly* music, now popular throughout Europe and North America as country music. Influenced by spirituals, blues and jazz, the black music which the South has given the world, country music is usually played on stringed instruments like the banjo, mandolin, guitar, fiddle and harmonica. Made by poor white sharecroppers and seasonally employed field-hands, this was music for hoedowns and barn raisings. Way down South, in Cajun country, the bayous of Louisiana, the rhythms of country music find their counterpart in the plaintive strains and stompin' beat of *Cajun music.* All this music is yet another example of how much the South, some of the most impoverished and isolated parts of it, has contributed to the world.

Historic Places

Throughout the South, signs proclaim *Historic Place* in black letters. Some of these indicate battlefields, a sure sign that the South is still traumatized by the Civil War. Southerners do tend to dwell in the past and treasure old houses. Coffee-table books abound on historic houses, James River or Natchez plantations and Colonial Williamsburg, a theme park overrun with tourists but instructive for lovers of period furnishings nonetheless. Where the Civil War wrought no devastation, 17th- and 18th-century houses, many still lived in by the descendants of the families who had them built, are open to the public at specified times. Gardens of centuries' old boxwood, camellias, and magnolias are smaller than their English counterparts but some are hauntingly beautiful. On the Eastern Shore of Virginia, you might spot a tiny sign to Eyre Hall a few miles north of the Chesapeake Bay Bridge and Tunnel. You'll drive miles along a

Trained on the south: Charlottesville court house

dusty avenue of papery crepe myrtles (in bloom in August) through fields hemmed in by ominously dark pine woods to reach a long, low white 17th-century house built of Atlantic cedar, with its original formal box garden. Tranquil in the westering sun that glints on Cherrystone Creek, this *plantation* is cherished by descendants of the Eyre family, whose members are still buried in raised graves in front of the orangery when they die.

Ku Klux Klan

In recent years the notorious hooded Klansmen led by *Grand Dragons* and their middle-class counterparts, *White Citizens' Councils,* haven't made headlines. The Klan, mainly disgruntled Southern white farmers, emerged in 1865 to terrify freed slaves with cross-burnings and lynchings until well into the 1930s. After World War II the Klan resurfaced, especially in Alabama and Mississippi, where Emmet Till, a black 14-year-old, was lynched in 1955. In 1964 the Klan bombed two dozen black churches and killed three Civil Rights workers, one a black from Mississippi. In March 1965 the Confederate flag waved proudly over the state capitol building in Montgomery, Alabama. After two former Grand Dragons of the Klan were exposed on the Oprah Winfrey Talk Show in 1988 for battling to acquire more local cable TV stations promoting racism in the South and southern Middle West, the Klan has managed to camouflage itself on web-sites with innocuous-sounding names where it is still spreading its message of hatred and white Aryan supremacy, invoking the First Amendment right of freedom of speech. The spate of black church-burnings that erupted across the South in 1997 may well have been instigated by the Klan in any one of its protean manifestations.

March to the Sea

Savannah, a major port city in southern Georgia, is one of the few large Southern cities to have retained its *antebellum* character. Although logistically important as a supply depot, it was spared the ravages of William Sherman's march through Georgia to the Atlantic in 1864 which left a swath of destruction 250 miles long through the state. Savannah had been evacuated by the time Sherman arrived there.

Mint Julep

Like no other long drink, an ice-cold *Mint Julep* has come to stand for the visitors' idea of the ideal summer refreshment in the South. Silver mugs or cut-crystal tumblers are chilled and filled with finely crushed ice, enough bourbon to cover the ice, sugar syrup to taste and served with 5 or 6 sprigs of fresh mint left to stick up above the rim. Georgia Mint Juleps substitute equal amounts of cognac and peach brandy for the bourbon and a Louisiana Mint Julep is made with rum. English travellers in the antebellum South were game to try it. In 1838, Captain Frederick Marryat noted in his diary: 'I must ... descant a little upon the mint-julep, as it is, with the thermometer at 38°C (100°F), one of the most delightful and insinuating potations that ever was invented.' However, in 1842 Charles Dickens found that the Mint Julep was a dangerously addictive potation, 'never to be thought of afterwards, in summer, by those who would preserve contented minds.'

Soul Food

Originally served in black homes, *Soul Food* today delights the souls of black and white alike. *Soul*, originally a term coined to describe music, now indiscriminately applies to everything ethnic throughout the US. If you prefer your vegetables crisp, bright green and lean, Southern greens cooked for a long time with pork are not for you. But who could resist *spoon bread*, a savoury corn meal soufflé served with other Southern delicacies like Southern fried chicken (home-cooked, naturally)?

Islands

Off the coasts of Virginia and Georgia are fascinating islands. Tangier Island in Chesapeake Bay is inhabited by whites who speak the *West Country dialect* of their Somerset, Devon and Cornish forebears and live in little, old pastel clapboard houses. To get there, take a day excursion boat from Crisfield, Maryland, or Onancock Virginia. Then, off the Georgia Coast, some of the magical Sea Islands are still inhabited by Gullahs, who speak *Geechee,* a hybrid of Elizabethan English and ancient African languages. The film *Daughters of the Dust,* is a moving tribute to the Gullahs. Cumberland Island, Sea Island, St. Simons Island and Sapelo are tropical places to enjoy which have escaped mass commercial development. The Greyfield Inn on Cumberland is set in white oaks, has big porch swings and superb modern Southern cuisine. There are miles of deserted beaches and wildlife abounds.

Tobacco

Throughout the US the antismoking campaign continues and

has consolidated most of its gains. You become aware of this on all domestic flights, when you are informed that smoking is not allowed. *No smoking!* is the rule in public buildings, on trains and in shopping malls and restaurants. Hotels often banish smokers to special rooms. Yet tobacco is important for the Southern economy. In Winston-Salem, North Carolina, R.J. Reynolds is still churning out cigarettes despite the drop in domestic consumption. A statue of R.J. Reynolds stands outside City Hall. Even the airport is named after the Reynolds family. The pervasive smell of tobacco leaves being cured hangs in the air and tobacco leaves are represented on the city's seal. More than 7,000 high-paying jobs in Winston-Salem depended on tobacco in 1999. The tobacco lobby has for years been effectively represented in the Senate by the redoubtable Jesse Helms of North Carolina, who loves to be photographed holding a cigarette. To improve its tarnished image, the tobacco industry is increasing its commitment to charities and civic welfare. R.J. Reynolds donated Winston-Salem US $16.9m between 1994 and 1999. Duke University in Durham, North Carolina, was founded and endowed by James B. Duke of the American Tobacco Company. Its Medical Center is Durham County's biggest employer. In the Piedmont region of eastern North Carolina, tobacco farmers have been hard hit by the decline in smoking. Many have changed to poultry and pig farming.

Literature

The glory of the South is her contribution to music and literature. The roll-call of writers is long: the playwright Tennessee Williams; the short story and novel writers Eudora Welty, Carson McCullers and Flannery O'Conner; the novelist Alice Walker, whose *The Color Purple* won a Pulitzer Prize; Zora Neale Hurston, one of the earliest American Black women academics; William Faulkner, awarded the Nobel Prize in 1949. Ellen Glasgow's novels about social and political conflicts in her native Virginia heralded feminism. And Edgar Allan Poe, whose influence on French Symbolism was so profound. Or John Kennedy Toole, who killed himself at thirty-two. His Swiftian *A Confederacy of Dunces,* set in New Orleans, is excruciatingly funny. There's always something both gothic and tragic about great Southern writers.

In the spirit of Marco Polo

Marco Polo was the first true world traveller. He travelled with peaceful intentions forging links between the East and the West. His aim was to discover the world, and explore different cultures and environments without changing or disrupting them. He is an excellent role model for the travellers of today and the future. Wherever we travel we should show respect for other peoples and the natural world.

Cuisine
Southern style

American? Caribbean? Cajun? Creole? French?
Southern cuisine is both regional and international

For starters: the Southern States are part of the US so here, as elsewhere throughout the country, the cooking is American. Visitors know that fast food of all kinds is available from nationwide chains serving pizzas, tacos, steaks and salads and fried chicken. However, this is only part of the picture. First, American cooking is multiethnic like the culture it reflects. Immigrants to America have all contributed to the cuisine of their new country. In addition, cooking in the South varies from region to region and not all variants are covered by the term *Southern style.* Even in modest restaurants serving simple fare, you'll usually be greeted by a sign requesting *Please wait to be seated,* before you are approached by your *host* or *hostess,* styled of course after expensive restaurants' *maître d'hôtel.* He or she will take you to a table, give you the menu and ask you whether you wish to see the wine list and whether you're lunching or dining.

Pizza, tacos and sushi
are fast food

Fast food, and not just hamburgers or hotdogs, can be a viable option. Pizzas come in all shapes and sizes, loaded with everything imaginable. American sandwiches make satisfying meals: hoagies (submarines), heroes, footlongs, double and triple deckers (the club sandwich with crispy bacon, lettuce, tomato and chicken is a triple decker). In the South you'll find chicken *by the (cardboard) bucket* - with 8, 12 or 16 pieces at restaurants or to go (takeaway).

All along the Southeastern seaboard, starting at Chesapeake Bay, fish and shellfish, collectively termed seafood, is incredibly plentiful, varied and cheap by European standards. Shellfish like fried oysters or clams is a roadside treat. Fast food chains even dispense lobster and fried shrimp in buckets, a satisfying meal with an ice-cold beer. If you love seafood and aren't afraid of eating raw oysters and other shellfish, why not go to a *raw bar,* a form of dégustation popular in cities and resorts? Safer – because the shellfish are cooked – and more delectable ways of enjoying

American oysters in good restaurants include oyster stew, devilled oysters, oysters Rockefeller and stuffed oysters.

In most cities and towns you'll come across Chinese and particularly Italian restaurants. There are also Greek, Vietnamese and Mexican eateries in many places. But, on the Southeastern seaboard, it's a safe bet you'll find most ethnic restaurants serving seafood and steaks too. You'll need help to fight your way through the jungle of Southern cuisine. Head for a drugstore and buy an armful of *Restaurant Guides* and even local papers with attractive and informative *Living* or *Lifestyle* sections and pages. And, at US $2.99, the venerable *Gourmet Magazine* is a reliable guide to cuisine and restaurants listed by state although restaurants in the Southern States rarely advertise in it. Look through the lifestyle magazines available where you are. Don't be misled by restaurant names. 'Antoine's' in New Orleans is not a greasy-spoon diner but a world-famous gourmet restaurant founded in the 19th century by M. Antoine Alciatore. Since Americans are obsessed with weight-watching and cholesterol, restaurants in all price brackets feature salads and fresh vegetables. At buffet-style salad bars you can browse through mountains of delicious greenery for a set price. Once you leave the fast-food scene, fish is grilled and vegetables like broccoli and slivered green beans are 'al dente', with a choice of side-dishes, including a baked potato or rice.

What you may think of as traditional *Southern style* cooking is mouth-watering, featuring delicacies like Smithfield ham (Virginia and South Carolina) and spoon bread. Queen Victoria had 6 Smithfield hams sent across the Atlantic to her per week. Along Chesapeake Bay and in the Carolinas, crab (usually blue crab) dishes like crab cakes, soft-shell crabs (in season), crabmeat baked in a cream sauce and topped with breadcrumbs, crab bisque or simply crab legs are peerless. If you're not careful, you'll put on pounds fast even if you turn down the beaten biscuits and avoid sticky Southern desserts like *pecan pie or Key lime pie,* which is deceptively zingy. Farmers' markets sell seasonal fruit and vegetables by the basket along highways.

Not *Southern style* but typical of the Deep South are the Florida Spanish-Cuban cuisine, the now upmarket French *Cajun* food of the Louisiana bayous and the *Creole* cuisine that have brought hot, spicy shrimp and chicken gumbo from the Caribbean to the Southeastern states.

In sections of Miami where Cuban Spanish is the prevailing language, tapas familiar from Spain are served as starters or with wine. Spanish paella is standard fare and fish soup is Zarzuela here instead of the chowder so beloved in the North Atlantic states. A Spanish delicacy popular in Florida is Seviche – which is rather like sushi – raw fish or shrimp, marinated in lemon juice, oil, parsley and garlic.

Bayou or *Cajun* cooking is basically French but draws on local freshwater fish like catfish and shellfish like crawfish (crayfish), known in the vernacular as mudbugs. There are Caribbean overtones, too. Cajun food can be so hot that you'll be glad for the rice served with it to neutralize the seasoning.

Cajun favourites with okra like *shrimp or chicken gumbo* and *jambalaya,* the paella introduced to New Orleans by the Spanish in the late 18th century, made with a mixture of ham, sausage, fish, shrimp and even conch, can be hot enough to make your eyes water.

Throughout the South, one of the two big daily meals is *breakfast.* Southern breakfasts, particularly at B & Bs, where *home cooking* reigns, can make even the classic English breakfast look meagre by comparison. In many places you'll even find the *Western Breakfast* with hashed brown potatoes. Because breakfast is so hearty, at *lunch* you'll only want a snack or a light meal like *soup and a sandwich,* or even just a sandwhich, perhaps the classic light *BLT – bacon, lettuce and tomato* – or, simpler and cheaper, a *tunafish salad sandwich.*

A *submarine (hoagy)* is French bread (a baguette) sliced lengthways, filled with bologna (baloney), iceberg lettuce and cheese, topped off with onion rings and liberally sprinkled with olive oil and coarse pepper. Remember, though, dinner is served early, usually by 6 pm, and rarely later than 9.30 pm.

Ice-water is served with lunch and dinner and your glass is replenished throughout the meal. You won't have to ask your waiter or waitress for it. Soft drinks and *iced tea* are also served with lots of ice. Beer is closer to English lager but is much lighter than any European beers. *Light beer* is lighter still. Although some states, notably Virginia, are experimenting with wine-growing, most wines you'll find in the South are either French or Italian, and often plonk at that. Strangely enough, the California wines on wine lists are usually more expensive than Italian and French wines, which tend to be in the lower range, while their California counterparts are the good ones and extremely expensive. The same holds for wines bought in supermarkets or package stores. California wine is reserved for connoisseurs.

For aficionados of *mixed drinks,* which, except for Bloody Marys, are full of sugar and cause horrendous hangovers, bartenders concoct planter's punch, mint juleps and martinis though margaritas and daiquirís (classic with lime but available in strawberry and banana) are often mixes straight out of the freezer. You don't have to be in Key West to savour Caribbean rum, notably from Barbados. During *happy hour,* usually between 5 pm and 7 pm, drinks are cheaper and hors d'oeuvres are included in the price or inexpensive.

Waiters and waitresses are invariably helpful and polite. Americans leave about 15 per cent of the bill as a *tip* discreetly tucked away underneath the rim of a plate because a service charge is not usually included on the bill.

Shopping
24 hours a day

*The American shopping mall
is a memorable experience*

Shop until you drop, that says it all without being disparaging. Americans love to shop because shopping brings variety and opportunities for socializing into their lives. *Shopping Malls* have had an enormous impact on *the downtown section* of countless cities. Malls are situated on the outskirts of big cities, somewhere at an intersection between several small towns. They offer all kinds of shops under one roof – several department store outlets, dozens of boutiques, many of them supraregional chains, some *drugstores* and bookshops as well as travel agents – and because so many of these centres have sprung up, stores downtown have lost customers. This in turn has accelerated the much decried decay of the *inner city.* There are signs, however, that the trend is being reversed. Inner cities are being *renewed* and young urban professionals are moving into restored *town houses,* bringing with them small shops and an attractive urban way of life.

Luxury, luxury – often more affordable than here in Palm Beach

Souvenirs are available at *news stands* in hotels, at theme parks ranging from Colonial Williamsburg to Disneyland, at airports and *shopping malls* and supermarkets. T-shirts, like Fruit of the Loom, once sold to farmers through the Sears Roebuck Catalog, are worn by young people everywhere. Sports shoes and jeans are cheaper in America. Those big *New Orleans coffee bowls* – for chicory-flavoured, milky coffee – will look nice on your breakfast table. Tinned and bottled spices are a low-cost option: Wagner's Creole seasoning, Luzianne Cajun seasoning and McCormick Old Bay for crab and chicken dishes. Delicious locally made preserves and honey are available at farmers' markets. Smalltown bookstores feature little recipe books, published locally, with those mouth-watering seafood dishes and cakes. What about music CDs? Consumer electronics, however, won't be compatible with European plugs and service guarantees are valid outside the US only for globally distributed products. Sales tax can be refunded at New Orleans airport so keep your Louisiana sales receipts.

Southerners love fairs and carnivals

Religious holidays are purely family affairs

The traditional American public festivals in America and the South are rodeos, horse fairs and *country fairs,* where racing (horse and cattle) and dances sweeten sales pitches. The *country fair* represents the survival of the English town market and horse fair and is a welcome diversion in the rural South. Peddlars, clowns, jugglers, circus artistes and musicians used to display their skills at them, and sideshows with freaks were a sine qua non in the non-PC (politically correct) days before World War II. In line with English and Scots-Irish Protestant tradition, religious holidays like Christmas and Easter are celebrated quietly in the family and at church. Miami, with its large Hispanic population, and New Orleans, settled by French Canadians, are predominantly Catholic and here the tradition is different, with Carnival celebrated as a colourful street festival. Even on religious holidays large stores and malls stay open. Easter Monday and Boxing Day after Christmas are not holidays in the hard-working US. Nor does the Whit weekend include Monday. National holidays may entail a long weekend, like *Memorial Day,* marking the onset of summer, Fourth of July and *Labor Day,* after which school starts. Both weekends are a chance for families to take a four-day break in the country or at the seashore. *Thanksgiving,* the US harvest festival, and *Christmas,* are occasions for family get-togethers. On *Halloween,* the US Guy Fawkes day, small children dress up and go from house to house with large bags, warning 'Trick or Treat'. Nashville and Memphis host *country music and rock festivals.* Football games between universities are the occasion for riotous partying in college towns.

PUBLIC HOLIDAYS

1 January: *New Year's Day*
3rd Monday in January: *Martin Luther King Day*
3rd Monday in February: *Presidents' Day*
Last Monday in May: *Memorial Day*
4 July Fourth of July – *Independence Day*

The Mother of all Carnivals: Mardi Gras stands for New Orleans

MARCO POLO SELECTION: FESTIVALS

1 Christmas
Best in Florida and best of all under the palms in Fort Lauderdale, far from snow, ice and the North Pole (pages 26 and 27)

2 Kentucky Derby
Superb thorough-breds, ladies in sensational elegant hats, tickets are hard to find but bad places are always available (page 26)

3 Mardi Gras
Before Ash Wednesday and Lent, a final burst of glorious fun, culminating in 'Fat Tuesday' with floats and Parades (page 26)

4 Memphis Musical Festival
Put on your blue suede shoes, Memphis is dedicated to the Fifties but is as modern as it comes (page 27)

1st Monday in September: *Labor Day*
2nd Monday in October: *Columbus Day*
11 November: *Veterans Day*
4th Thursday in November: *Thanksgiving*
25 December ★ *Christmas*
Banks, public offices, post offices and many shops are closed on the above days.

FESTIVALS

January
❖ *Orange Bowl Festival* The high point of the football season; eight days of parades and festivals. *From 1 January, Miami*

February
Silver Spurs Rodeo Like the Wild West, central Florida is horse country. *3rd weekend, Kissimmee*
★ ❖ *Mardi Gras* – called fat Tuesday instead of Shrove Tuesday – in New Orleans, surpassed only by Carnival in Rio. *Calle Ocho Festival* in Miami, when Cubans in exile celebrate Carnival in their streets with Samba and Salsa. *Partying stops on Ash Wednesday, which can be as late as early March*

March
St. Patrick's Day Catholic Irish celebrate their patron saint with a huge parade. *On the Sunday closest to 17 March, in Savannah, Georgia*

April
Great Passion Play The last days before the Crucifixion as a Passion Play with camels, horses and over 200 players. *Last Fri in the month until last Sat in Oct, daily except Mon and Thurs in Eureka Springs, Arkansas*

May
★ *Kentucky Derby* The big race – Ascot and Newmarket rolled into one, *1st Sat, Louisville, Kentucky. Spoleto Festival USA* Theatre, dance, jazz, opera, symphonic and chamber music – 17

26

days of it. *End of the month, Charleston, South Carolina*

June

International Country Music Fan Fair The biggest festival with Country bands. *Mid-month, Nashville, Tennessee*

August

❖ *Mountain Dance and Folk Festival* Fiddlers, square dancers and ballad singers perform for a whole month. *Asheville, North Carolina*

September

★ *Memphis Music Festival* Jazz, Blues and Rock in their traditional haunts in legendary Beale Street, where Elvis Presley's career was launched. *All month, Memphis*

October

Halloween Dressed up in costumes, kids knock on doors and call: *Trick or Treat!* Practical jokes, like hoisting porch furniture up telephone poles, are played on people who don't put candies into the big bags. *Bobbing for Apples* in a tub of water is evening fun. *31 Oct, everywhere*

December

★ *Christmas* Great fun under the tropical sun with sweating Santa Clauses and artificial snow on plastic Christmas trees. Festively decorated yachts replace sleds at the *Winterfest and Boat Parade*, Florida's bigger and brasher version of fishing villages in Southwest England with their Christmas harbour decorations. *Fort Lauderdale, Florida*

Howdy? Hah, y'awl!

English may be your mother tongue, but you haven't understood a word? Linguists love the South. In Miami many people speak Spanish as their first language. In New Orleans and the Bayou country of Louisiana, a lot of Creole French is spoken and not just on restaurant menus. In Savannah and the Sea Islands of Georgia, Geechee, a blend of Elizabethan English and African languages, still keeps outsiders guessing. Southerners of English, Scots-Irish and African descent speak with various versions of the *southern drawl*, which the English actress Vivian Leigh mastered for Gone with the Wind. *Howdy or hi, y'awl*, instead of *How do you do? The old children's counting rhyme – Eenie, meenie, minie, mo*, that used to go on to *catch a Nigger by his toe* is no longer acceptable as it is not PC, and indeed is crassly racist. But *y'awl – you all –* certainly don't need to be told that. Euphemisms are thick on the ground among the poorer elderly residents of small towns. Taking the name of the Lord in vain has always been frowned on in the deeply religious South. To express surprise or consternation, don't call out *by God*, say *by Gosh* instead. And *damned*, turns into *darned*. *Gee, whiz*, as dated as it sounds, is still used by people who no longer realize that this expletive really means Jesus' wounds. Forsooth!

Where the South begins

Wild, deserted Atlantic beaches, the Appalachians and the Old South

The sprawling conurbation consisting of cities that have grown together all down the Eastern seaboard as far as Washington comes abruptly to an end at the District of Columbia and the nation's capital. South and east of the Potomac, in Northern and Eastern Shore Virginia, cities and even towns are few and far between. Virginia and the Carolinas have a lot in common. This is not the *Deep South.* Although summers can be surprisingly muggy here, there's often a breeze off Chesapeake Bay and the Atlantic. The Eastern Shore of Virginia and the Carolinas are notable for long, in places deserted, beaches and barrier islands. The shore is flat and covered with pine barrens. Autumn and winter storms can wreak havoc with dunes and beaches, leaving them unrecognizably changed from one year to the next. To the west of the arc formed by the state capitals – Richmond, Raleigh and Columbia – the countryside becomes

rolling and hilly. From an elevation of 1,000 to 2,000 m in the Blue Ridge Mountains, part of the long Appalachian system, there are superb views out across the flat land.

Tobacco is grown in the Carolinas, especially in the Piedmont, where the mountains of Virginia and North Carolina begin. These farms are small, nothing like the old tobacco plantations or the cotton plantations further south. However, be careful about judging distances in this lovely, rolling country. If you're planning to drive from northern Virginia to the southern border of South Carolina, you'll be spending a long day in your car, not counting rest stops and detours to explore.

As always in the US, you'll have to come to a definite decision. Where do you really want to go? Do you want to explore the magnificent dunes of the Outer Banks, the barrier islands, with their wild horses and flat-bottomed ferries? Or do you want to stay inland and take the Skyline Drive, going on from Shenandoah to Great Smoky National Park?

Neo-Classical charm:
the historic section of Charleston

Don't forget to visit historic places and old houses and towns. Their history unites the three states usually known as the *Old South*. Virginia, the *Old Dominion*, was the earliest British colony in the New World. In April 1607 George Percy noted in his *Observations:* 'fair meadows, and goodly tall trees, with such fresh waters as almost ravished ... the senses of men set ashore near the mouth of the Chesapeake Bay.' However, Percy's early glimpse of paradise proved illusory. As early as 1585 Sir Walter Raleigh had attempted to plant a colony on the island of Roanoke off the North Carolina coast and one planted in 1587 succumbed to Indian attacks and disease. In recent years archaeological excavations have begun to shed light on Roanoke and other unsuccessful attempts at establishing colonies. North Carolina was settled from Virginia. Granted a charter in 1663 as a buffer zone between Florida, where the Spanish had had colonies since the 16th century, and the French in Louisiana; South Carolina was not settled by the English until 1670.

The last Southern colony of the original Thirteen Colonies to ratify the Constitution (not until November 1789), North Carolina, with Virginia, Arkansas and Tennessee, joined the Confederacy as a member of the second secession.

South Carolina, whose economy depended more on rice and indigo plantations, made it the biggest importer of slaves and was

Hotel and restaurant prices

Hotels

Category 1: luxury hotels and cottages over US $120
Category 2: good hotels under US $120
Category 3: unpretentious hotels and motels under US $80
Prices quoted are for two people in a double room. Single rooms usually cost the same or not much less. Children can usually sleep with their parents for no additional charge. Nearly all hotels and motels have swimming pools as well as telephones and television in all rooms. Inexpensive Best Western, Days Inn or Econo Lodge motels are usually on highway exits and near feeder roads to highways.

Restaurants

Category 1: over US $50
Category 2: US $30-US $50
Category 3: under US $30
Prices are for an evening meal with soup or starter, a main course and dessert.

Important abbreviations

Av.	Avenue	**Hwy.**	Highway
Bd.	Boulevard	**Mt.**	Mount
Dr.	Drive	**Rd.**	Road
Grove St./	Crove St., corner	**St.**	Street or Saint
Pine St.	Pine Street	**Sts.**	Streets

MARCO POLO SELECTION: VIRGINIA, NORTH AND SOUTH CAROLINA

1. **Appalachian Trail**
The legendary trail through the Appalachian System (page 43)
2. **Charleston**
A gracious 18th- and 19th-century city in the Old South: South Carolina (page 33)
3. **Colonial Williamsburg**
A theme park, the cradle of the American Revolution (page 39)
4. **Outer Banks**
Long, lonely islands off the North Carolina coast (page 40)
5. **Sheraton Jefferson Hotel**
A 19th-century luxury hotel in Richmond, Virginia (page 43)
6. **University of Virginia**
Founded and designed by Thomas Jefferson in Charlottesville, Virginia (page 36)

the first to break with the Union. It paid dearly for it. General William T. Sherman was writing by June 1864: '... I see no signs of a remission till one or both the armies are destroyed. ... I begin to regard the death and mangling of a couple thousand men as a small affair, a kind of morning dash – and it may well be that we become so hardened.' In February 1865 Columbia, the capital of South Carolina, was torched.

ARLINGTON/ ALEXANDRIA

(105/D1) These two adjoining towns in northern Virginia are really suburbs of Washington, D.C., separated from it only by the broad Potomac. Arlington is famous for *Arlington National Cemetery,* where American soldiers from many wars lie buried as well as Supreme Court justices and statesmen, most notably John F. Kennedy, who was assassinated in 1963, and his wife Jackie. An 'eternal flame' burns on their grave. The grave of the Unknown Soldier is on the spot where the gallant commander of the Confederate forces, General Robert E. Lee, had his rose garden. Lee's old plantation house, *Arlington House,* was confiscated after the Civil War but has been restored and opened to the public. From Arlington Cemetery there are fine views of the Neo-Classical buildings and monuments of the capital city across the river. Every hour, on the hour – in summer every half hour – the Guard changes at the *Tomb of the Unknown Soldier.* This is an impressively solemn ceremony conducted by soldiers of the 3rd U.S. Infantery Regiment. *Daily 8 am–5 pm, Apr–Sept till 7 pm (Arlington Cemetery), 9.30 am–4.30 pm, Apr–Sept till 6 pm (Arlington House); admission free; entrance to the cemetery at the western end of Arlington Memorial Bridge, Metro station: Arlington Cemetery*

Right outside Arlington Cemetery stands the *U.S. Marine Corps War Memorial.* Better known as the National Iwo Jima Memorial Monument, it was designed after the prize-winning photo taken by Joseph Rosenthal of Marines struggling to raise the American flag on Mount Suribachi on the Japanese island of Iwo Jima.

Also close by is the *Pentagon,* a colossal five-sided structure with offices for thousands of civilian and military workers in the Defence Department. This is the world's largest government office building. *Guided tours Mon–Fri 9 am–5 pm; admission free*

Alexandria, next to Arlington, was once a tobacco port on the Potomac. The *Old Town* was founded in 1749. Visitors enjoy walking through its cobbled streets. A stroll through Alexandria might begin at the *Alexandria Tourist Council* in *Ramsay House (221 King St.),* the oldest house in town and home of the city's first mayor, William Ramsay. There you'll find lots of informative brochures and city maps. Particularly notable are the fine *Carlyle House,* historic *Old Gadsby's Tavern,* frequented by George Washington, and a handsome terrace of *captains' houses* in *Prince Street.*

RESTAURANT

Old Gadsby's Tavern
A tavern as it looked in the 18th century. Waitresses and waitors, dressed in 18th century costume, serve hearty American fare. *138 N Royal St., Alexandria, Tel. 703/548-12 88, category 3*

HOTELS

Princely B & B
Bed & Breakfast agency for approx 30 lovely 18th- and 19th-century houses in Alexandria, the delightful alternative to staying at a hotel. Minimum stay: two days. *819 Prince St., Alexandria, Tel. and Fax 703/683-21 59, mostly category 2*

Quality Inn Iwo Jima
A motel close to Washington with a swimming pool and restaurant. *142 rooms, 1501 Arlington Bd., Arlington, Tel. 703/524-50 00, Fax 522-54 84, category 2*

SURROUNDING AREA

Mount Vernon   (105/D1-2)
The country house that belonged to the first president, George Washington, which he started to build in 1754 and where he died in 1799. A handsome late Geor-

Popular with the locals: Myrtle Beach in South Carolina

gian house, it is a National Monument, visited by millions of Americans. Most visitors come at weekends and during the summer. *25 km to the south on the George Washington Memorial Parkway and Mount Vernon Memorial Hwy.* Great fun to go by excursion boat on the Potomac: departures *daily 9 am and 2 pm; Pier 4, 6th St./Water St., Washington, D.C.*

CHARLESTON

☛ **City Map on page 108**

(104/B6) ★ Its location alone at the confluence of the rivers Ashley and Cooper would make it attractive. Considered the most beautiful city in the United States and one which continues to entrance British travel writers and other visitors, Charleston is sophisticated and elegant. About 160 km to the north is a popular seaside resort *Myrtle Beach,* and it's about the same distance to Savannah, Georgia, along a marshy coast with memorably beautiful islands. In both Charleston and Savannah and on the islands in between, the seafood is superb. And now a look at this enchanting city: 1,500 listed buildings in an area covering a mere 10 square km – all those fine 17th-, 18th- and 19th-century houses, many of them in delicate pastel tints. Charleston is now a place to be quietly lived in and loved. By the 1680s the port, Charles Town Landing, named after Charles II, was consolidating the agrarian economy. Slave ships landed here, and cotton and rice were laden to be shipped to Bristol and Liverpool. Even during the 19th century, before the Civil War, Liverpool cotton merchants based their operations in Charleston. In the 17th

and 18th centuries, Charleston was, after Philadelphia, the biggest port on the Eastern seaboard. In the 18th-century *Huguenots* taught French to planters' sons.

SIGHTS

Drayton Hall

Built in 1738 on the Ashley River and left much as it was, even when electricity and modern heating were built in, the house now stands empty, the absence of furnishings making it a good place to study Palladian Georgian architecture. *Daily 10 am–3 pm, 1 Mar–31 Oct till 4 pm; admission US $8; on Hwy. S Carolina 61, 15 km north of Charleston; Tel. 803/766-01 88*

Edmonston-Alston House

A splendid two-story example of America's answer to Regency, built in 1826, with lovely ☙ views of the harbour. It is furnished and appointed in the Directory style, an American variant of Neo-Classical Empire with a decidedly Greek look. *Tues–Sat 10 am–4.30 pm, Sun, Mon 1.30 pm–4.30 pm; admission US $7, Combination ticket with five other sites US $29; 21 E Battery; Tel. 803/722-71 71*

Fort Sumter National Monument

Built on a man-made island between 1829 and 1860, the Fort is important as the place where the first shots of the Civil War were fired. On 12 April 1861, Confederates fired from the shore on Fort Sumter because Union soldiers were stationed there. They surrendered after two days. This marks the beginning of modern, total warfare fought with modern heavy artillery. *Excursions by boat* *take 2.5 hours with a tour of the harbour: times change, depending on the season of the year; Fort Sumter Tours, Charleston City Marina, 17 Lockwood Bd.; Tel. 803/722-16 91; Boat ticket US $10, free admission to the Fort*

Heyward-Washington House
Finished in 1772, the stately residence of Thomas Heyward, one of the signers of the Declaration of Independence, was, briefly, also the home of the first President, George Washington. *Mon–Sat 10 am–5 pm, Sun 1 pm–5 pm, closed on holidays; admission US $6; 87 Church St.; Tel. 803/722-03 54*

Huguenot Church
By the late 17th century, French Huguenots fleeing religious persecution had settled in South Carolina, mainly on the Cooper River. They went to Charleston by boat to divine service in this Neo-Gothic church, built in 1845. *Mon–Fri 10 am–4 pm, Sat 10 am–12 am except national holidays; admission free; 136 Church St.*

Joseph Manigault House
Finished in 1803 in the Adam style, the grand main house was built on a parallelogram-shaped ground pan with two crescent-shaped bays on the ends. Louis XVI motifs recall the French Huguenot ancestry of the original owners. *Mon–Sat 10 am–5 pm, Sun 1 pm–5 pm, closed on holidays; admission US $6; 350 Meeting St.; Tel. 803/722-29 96*

Nathaniel Russell House
Finished in the Neo-Classical Adam style in 1808, this was the house of a rich tradesman. A remarkable flying staircase spirals up three floors without visible support. *Mon–Sat 10 am–5 pm, Sun 2 pm–5 pm; admission US $4, on a combination ticket including five other historic buildings US $29; 51 Meeting St.; Tel. 803/724-84 81*

St. Michael's Episcopal Church
Built in 1751, this church boasts a Dorian portal and a spire 60 m high. It is one of the few urban churches in the US to have retained its original appearance and appointments since it was consecrated. *Mon–Fri 9 am–5 pm, Sat 9 am–12 am; admission free; Meeting St./Broad St.*

The Colony House
The best seafood restaurant in Charleston, and that is saying something, this one is really special. Do try the crab dishes, which are specialities of the Southeastern seaboard. *Daily dinner, lunch Mon–Sat, closed on holidays, 35 Prileau St., Tel. 803/723-34 24, category 2*

82 Queen
Enjoy seafood specialities of the Southeastern seaboard like crab cakes or grilled duck and stuffed lobster in a stylishly elegant ambience. Nearly a century old, the building is resplendent in pretty pink stucco. *Daily. Dinner/lunch, 82 Queen St., Tel. 803/723-75 91, category 1*

Thomas Elfe Workshop
Next to the house (also open to the public) of the cabinet-maker Thomas Elfe, who furnished so many Charleston man-

sions, this small workshop is full of the typical small artefacts once in daily use and now so hard to find. *Mon–Fri 10 am–5 pm, Sat 10 am–1 pm, 54 Queen St.*

HOTELS

In Charleston, too, staying at a Bed & Breakfast in an old house is the best way of absorbing the atmosphere of the *Old South* . Information and booking: *Historic Charleston B & B, 43 Legore St., Tel. 803/722-66 06, Fax 722 -97 73*

Heart of Charleston Quality Inn
In the historic part of town, a hotel with rooms in the Southern tradition of gracious living, some with balconies. Swimming pool. *126 rooms, 125 Calhoun St., Tel. and Fax 803/722-33 91, category 1*

Kings Courtyard Inn
Where 19th-century antebellum plantation owners stayed whenever they went to Charleston on business. Located at the heart of the shopping section, a block from the Old City Market. Sleep under a canopy in a four-poster bed. Parquet floors and Persian rugs, some rooms with handsome fireplaces. *46 rooms, 198 King St., Tel. 803/723-70 00, Fax 720-26 08, category 1*

Two Meeting Street
The finest Bed & Breakfast with individually decorated and appointed rooms. Honeymoon suites with fireplace and veranda. Price includes breakfast and afternoon sherry. As in nearly all B & Bs in the US, no smoking. *9 rooms, 2 Meeting St., Tel. 803/723-73 22, no Fax, categories 1–2*

INFORMATION

Area Visitor Information Center
The best address for city maps and information brochures. *375 Meeting St., Tel. 803/853-80 00, no Fax*

CHARLOTTESVILLE

(104/C2) The University of Virginia, founded by Thomas Jefferson, boasts the most beautiful campus in the US. Quadrangles, red brick buildings, terraced *lawns* and serpentine walls form a harmonious whole. Jefferson's Rotunda is modelled on the Roman Pantheon. Close by is Monticello, which Jefferson, an architect of American independence, designed for himself.

SIGHTS

Monticello
Palladian at its most playful: the exterior of Jefferson's house is Classical in style. The interior, however, conceals Jeffersonian conceits. Mirrors in the hall reflect upside down. Not only a great statesman, Jefferson was a true son of the Enlightenment. Scholar, natural scientist, architect and gourmet, he designed his lifestyle in all details. Practical furniture as well as idiosyncratic inventions like a dual-pen polygraph for copying documents fill the house. As enlightened as he was, Jefferson was still a slave-holder. His illicit union with a slave woman has been a boon to biographers. Next to the big house is *Mulberry Row,* quarters for 200 slaves. *Daily 9 am–4.30 pm; admission US $8; 5 km south of Charlottesville on Hwy. VA 53*

Jefferson's Palladian Monticello in hilly Virginia

University of Virginia

★ In 1976 the University of Virginia was declared the most handsome set of public buildings in the US. The *Lawn* surrounded by colonnades at the centre of campus is the best place to view the whole. Students still live in the rooms there. One room is open to the public, No. 13, which was occupied by Edgar Allan Poe. He was expelled from the university in 1826. His father refused to send him the money for his tuition fees because he had amassed gambling debts. A stay at the military Academy at West Point in 1830 ended for this Southern gentleman in a dishonourable discharge. *Daily 10 am–4 pm; 45-minute guided tours free of charge; from the Rotunda*

Michie Tavern

Here you'll feast on Southern fried chicken, black-eyed peas, pan-fried tomatoes and cornbread: traditional Southern cuisine. *Daily 11.30 am–3 pm, Hwy. VA 53, 2.5 km beyond Monticello, category 3*

Best Western Mount Vernon

A quiet motel with a lovely view of the mountains. *110 rooms, at the intersection of Business 29 and US 29-250, Tel. 804/296-55 01, Fax 977-62 49, category 3*

Boar's Head Inn

Colonial elegance. Tennis courts. The restaurant serves good, traditional American food. Dress code (ladies in skirts and gentlemen in jackets, please!) *173 rooms, US 250 west of the Bypass US 29-250, Tel. 804/296-21 81, Fax 972-60 24, category 1, restaurant open daily 7 am–9.30 pm*

FREDERICKSBURG

(105/D2) The biggest town between Washington, D.C., and the capital of Virginia, Richmond, has retained much of its charm. In the 18th century Fredericksburg was a major river port to which tobacco and other plantation goods were shipped on the Rappahannock. There are quite a few 18th- and 19th-century houses along the river. *(go to the Visitor Center, 706 Caroline St., Tel. 703/373-17 76 to buy tickets for guided walks).* Of great strategic importance during the Civil war due to its location, Fredericksburg suffered devastating losses. More than 100,000 soldiers died in battles in and around Fredericksburg. At Fredericksburg *National Battlefield Park* there is a museum with Civil War memorabilia. You can also take a guided *Audio-Tour (US $2.75 for cassette and recorder),* which takes three hours. *Daily 9 am–5 pm; 1013 Lafayette Bd., south of town; Tel. 703/373-61 22; admission free*

GREAT SMOKY MOUNTAINS NATIONAL PARK

☛ **Map on pages 108/109**

(103/D-E3-4) A vast, quiet national park in the Appalachian with ridges rising to over 2,000 m. The smoke hanging over this virgin forest comes from a blend of steam and volatile oils released by trees and other plants. They can also be reached from North Carolina, via *Asheville* and *Cherokee.* (more on this on page 84.)

JAMESTOWN, WILLIAMSBURG AND YORKTOWN

(105/D2) The three towns are on a peninsula at the confluence of the rivers James and York, about an hour's drive east of *Richmond,* Virginia's capital. This *Historic Tri-angle* was originally a group of 17th-century towns which have been reconstructed as theme parks, here termed *living museums.* If theme parks are not to your taste, even educational ones, be warned. Service personnel is dressed in Colonial costume to engage in Colonial pursuits. Why not avoid busloads of schoolchildren and the general crush by driving down the James River to visit Carter's Grove plantation (1755), with its restored slave quarter, or upriver to Berkeley (1726), Westover (1730: open 5 days a year) or Shirley (1723), with its Queen Anne forecourt?

Hardly anything is left of the original *Jamestown,* the first permanent English Crown colony in North America. On 26 April 1607 (old calendar), three ships bringing 30 colonists and 75 indentured servants landed at the mouth of the James River. Led to expect paradise, at least 6,000 of 7,000 colonists who tried to settle here were dead within a decade, most of them in the first year after they landed. At first friendly, the Indians under Powhatan were provoked by the settlers' behaviour to attack them in 1622 and 1644. The settlers were indeed their own worst enemy. They shipped tonnes of tobacco back to England but felt inadequately protected and supported by the Crown. In 1675 they protested against what they regarded as cavalier treatment by burning down the settlement. All that remains at the *Jamestown National Historic Site* is the tower of a brick church, foundations and streets. *Jamestown Settlement* next to the town is a complete archaeological reconstruction. The museum

Looks like Washington, D.C.: the Capitol in Columbia, South Carolina

is instructive on the history of the settlement, with outstanding social and economic background material. You can visit two groups of reconstructed buildings. First, there is *Powhatan's* settlement, where Indian maidens clad in doeskin weave make pots. The other is a reconstruction of the 15 huts constituting *James Fort,* where 17th-century implements are used for work. Three ships, the Discovery, the Godspeed and the Susan Constant, are full-scale replicas of the originals which brought the colonists from England. In 1985 the Godspeed sailed to England. *Daily 9 am–5 pm; admission US $9.75, children between 6 and 12 US $4.75, Combination ticket includes Yorktown Victory Center US $13.25 and US $6.50; east of Richmond on Colonial Parkway, branching off Interstate I 64*

After Jamestown burned, the settlers who had not yet succumbed to disease and Indian raids settled at *Middle Plantation*, which became the capital of the colony in 1699, when it was renamed *Williamsburg* after King William III. Virginia grew into the richest of the American colonies. The *Capitol* was built in 1704 and in 1720 the impressive *Governor's Palace.* Virginia was the birthplace of American independence and republican ideals of a state with an elected head of state rather than a king. At the *College of William and Mary,* founded in 1693, and in the Williamsburg taverns, Patrick Henry, Thomas Jefferson, James Monroe, George Mason and the law professor George Wythe hatched out the ideas that led to Patrick Henry's stirring pronouncement *Give me liberty or give me death,* the Declaration of Independence, the War of Independence and the founding of the United States. Loyalists to the Crown moved to Richmond, later the Confederate capital and still Virginia's.

In 1934 restoration of ★ *Colonial Williamsburg* – funded by the oil billionaire John D. Rockefeller – made it the first historical theme park in the US. It is not surprising that President Ronald Reagan, well aware of the importance of a telegenic setting, chose Williamsburg as a Summit venue. More than 1 million visitors a year confirm the veteran movie actor's choice. About 150 reconstructed or restored buildings show what life was like in Colonial Virginia between 1698 and 1780. Craftsmen ply the 17th-century tools of their trade, bakers bake bread as they did in the Colonies and waitresses are dressed as tavern wenches. In the evening the Revolutionary War Fife and Drum Corps parades jauntily in the streets. Drugstores and jewellers' shops, however, stock modern inventory. Over it all looms the *Capitol* at the eastern end of Duke of Gloucester Street and the *Governor's Palace* at the northern end of Palace Green. Thomas Jefferson, Patrick Henry and other Revolutionary War firebrands met in the *Raleigh Tavern* to plot rebellion. Insurrectionists caught by spies in the service of the Crown were thrown into the *Public Gaol* to cool their heels. *Mon–Fri 9 am–5 pm, Sat, Sun 8.30 am–6 pm, in peak season open longer in the evenings; three types of tickets: Patriot's Pass (valid for 1 year): US $34, children between 6 and 12*

US $19; Colonist's Pass (2 consecutive days): US $30/US $17; Basic Ticket (1 day): US $26/US $15, not valid for the Governor's Palace, additional ticket for US $17/ US $10; east of Richmond on Colonial Parkway; Tel. 757/220-76 45 or 800/447-86 79

As a place-name *Yorktown* means more than just the town. On 17 October 1781 the British under General Cornwallis were defeated on land near Yorktown by the Revolutionary forces led by Washington and Comte de Rochambeau with 6,700 French soldiers, covered at sea by the naval squadron commanded by the French Admiral de Grasse. Yorktown was the decisive victory over the British. The *Visitor Center* at the site of the land battle is highly informative on this. *(daily 9 am–5 pm; admission free),* in the *Yorktown Victory Center,* built to resemble a Continental Army camp, you can imagine how Washington's ragged forces felt when the tide of Revolution turned in their favour. *admission US $6.75/US $3.25, Combination Ticket with Jamestown see above.*

RESTAURANTS

In the *Historic Triangle* you won't find much more than diners and snackbars with fast food. Notable exceptions are the Old World taverns along Duke of Gloucester Street in *Colonial Williamsburg,* which serve 17th- and 18th century fare in recreations of pre-Revolutionary war inns.

Trellis Cafe

A really good eatery with salads and light sandwiches as well as light American nouvelle cuisine.

A lovely shady patio. *Daily lunch and dinner, Duke of Gloucester St., outside the historic section of Williamsburg in Merchants Square, Tel. 804/229-86 10, category 2*

HOTELS

There aren't even that many good hotels in the *Historic Triangle.* At US $80–US $100, the motels near Colonial Williamsburg are overpriced. Escape across the Bay to the Eastern Shore and stay at B & Bs in old houses.

Royce
A spacious modern building designed to fit in well with Colonial Williamsburg. *313 rooms, 415 Richmond Rd., Tel. 804/229-40 20, Fax 220-15 60, category 1*

Williamsburg Inn
A charming Colonial-style inn with cosy but elegant rooms at the heart of the historic section. *102 rooms, Francis St., Tel. 804/229-10 00, Fax 220-70 96, category 1*

INFORMATION

Williamsburg Visitor Center
Information, maps, tickets, hotel bookings. *Colonial Parkway/VA 132, Tel. 804/229-10 00, no Fax, Mon–Fri 9 am–5 pm*

OUTER BANKS

(105/E3–4) ★ They're only sandbanks but what magnificent sandbanks they are! Barrier islands extend from southern Maryland, down the Virginia Eastern Shore and all along the North Carolina coast as far as *Cape Lookout* near *Beaufort,*

North Carolina (don't mix it up with Beaufort, South Carolina). Here you'll find 300 km of beach, parts of it still pristine and entirely deserted. Dunes are staggeringly big – among the world's highest. Here and further south, bridges connect islands with the mainland. Ferries ply between some islands. One accessible from the north via US 158 by a low bridge is *Bodie Island,* with three towns that run into each other: *Kitty Hawk, Kill Devil Hills* and *Nag's Head.* Along the highway and, parallel with it, on *Beach Road,* there are restaurants, motels and summer houses galore. The next island, *Roanoke Island,* is also linked to the mainland by a bridge: US Hwy. 64-264. A second attempt at founding an English colony on Roanoke failed in 1587. The settlers mysteriously vanished from this lost colony. A restored earthwall doesn't attract many visitors. *Mid-June–Labor Day daily 9 am–8.15 pm, Labor Day–mid-June daily 9 am–5 pm; admission free; 5 km north of Manteo on Hwy. US 64*

The next islands to the south are *Hatteras* and *Ocracoke,* which are part of a nature reserve, *Cape Hatteras National Seashore.* On the northern tip of Ocracoke, you can walk through *Pea Island National Wildlife Refuge* on a network of trails and watch birds. The western shore of the island is fringed with salt marshes but the eastern shore boasts sand dunes and long beaches. Stop anywhere along *Hwy. 12* and walk to them. The village of Ocracoke marks the southern tip of the island. Ferries run between Hatteras and

Ocracoke because there are no bridges. *The crossing takes 40 minutes, leaving from both islands between 7 am–6.30 pm on the hour and half hour. Cars roll off in reverse to the order in which they rolled on*

SIGHTS

Wright Brothers National Memorial

Orville Wright's diary tells us this about the first engine-powered flight on 17 December 1903 that the machine suddenly climbed 10 feet and then, just as suddenly, dived down again when he moved the stick ... all this in about 12 seconds. His brother Wilbur had asked onlookers not to look serious but to smile and applaud. An imposing site on a high sand dune recalls the experiment that was to change the world. Everything is explained in the *Visitor Center,* where there is also a replica of the first plane called The Flyer; the original is in the Washington National Air and Space Museum. *Mid-June–Labor Day daily 9 am–6 pm, otherwise 9 am–5 pm; admission US $2; on Hwy. US 158 Bypass, milemarker 8, Kill Devil Hill; Tel. 919/441-74 30*

RESTAURANTS

The Back Porch

Deliciously prepared fresh vegetables and a cornucopia of local fish and shellfish are served on a typical, screened in porch. *May–Oct daily 5.30 pm–10 pm; Ocracoke, on Hwy. NC 1324, 1 km north of the ferry landing; Tel. 919/928-64 01, category 2*

Bubba's Bar-B-Q

❖ This is how barbecue should look and taste: succulent spareribs, beef, chops and chicken grilled over hickory-scented charcoal while you watch. *Daily 11 am–10 pm; Hatteras, 10 km south of the lighthouse in Frisco Village, Tel. 919/995-54 21, category 3*

Channel Bass Restaurant

In a nautical setting – rather like a captain's cabin – superb locally caught fish and regional seafood dishes. *Apr–Nov daily 5 pm–9 pm; Hatteras, on Hwy. NC 12 north after Hatteras Village, Tel. 919/986-22 60, category 3*

HOTELS

Duke of Dare Motor Lodge

A basic motel with a pool and cable TV. *57 rooms, Roanoke, Hwy. US 64-264 in Manteo, Tel. 919/473-21 75, no Fax, category 3*

Island Inn

The most beautiful place to stay on the Outer Banks, built in 1901 of wood salvaged from a shipwreck, the building was used as both a school and an officers' club. The rooms with the best views are in the Crows Nest. The annex is like a motel. Pool and restaurant. *37 rooms, 2 cottages, closed mid-Nov–late Feb, Ocracoke, Hwy. NC 12, Tel. 919/928-43 51, Fax 928-43 52, categories 2–3*

Sea Gull Motel

Right on the beach with a choice of apartments and rooms with cooking facilities *(efficiencies).* Pool. *45 rooms, Hatteras, Hwy. NC 12, Tel. 919/986-25 50, Fax 986-25 25, categories 2–3*

Outer Banks
Chamber of Commerce
Mon–Fri 9 am–4.30 pm, Box 1757, Kill Devil Hill, NC 27948, Tel. 919/441-81 44, Fax 441-03 38

RICHMOND

(105/D2) During the Civil War Richmond was the *capital of the Confederacy* between May 1861 and April 1865. After the war large parts of the city were demolished, allegedly a scorched-earth policy of the fleeing Confederates who did not want to leave weapons and tobacco, a va-luable crop, for the Yankees. Tobacco is still Virginia's main crop. Modern Richmond is a banking centre, boasting skyscrapers in the usual style of small American cities. Patricia Cornwell's crime novels are set here.

SIGHTS

On *Court End* hill there are a number of stately *antebellum*-mansions, which are not open to the public.

Virginia State Capitol
The Capitol, since 1788 the seat of the Virginia Assembly, the state legislature, is at the heart

Far from the madding crowd: Cape Hatteras

42

of the city. From the columned portal the ◆ view encompasses the entire city of Richmond. The francophile Thomas Jefferson, a prolific architect, also helped to design the building, modelling it on the Maison Carrée in Nîmes. The only statue of George Washington made during the first president's lifetime stands in the Rotunda. *Daily 9 am–5 pm; admission free; Capitol Square*

MUSEUM

Museum of the Confederacy

Two blocks north of the Capitol, the museum gives a balanced account of the Civil War. Of course emphasis is put on the battles and the leaders of the Confederacy. Next to the museum is what is known as the *White House of the Confederacy,* the Neo-Classical mansion which was the residence of the Confederacy's only president, Jefferson Davis. *Mon–Sat 10 am–5 pm, Sun noon–5 pm, museum and White House; admission to each US $ 4; 1201 E Clay St.; Tel. 804/649-18 61*

HOTEL

Sheraton Jefferson

★ A luxury hotel dating from 1895. The Sheraton Jefferson is worth a visit even if you don't stay there simply for its fountains, rotunda and flying staircase. If you do stay here, you'll be treated to all the amenities of late 19th-century Southern gracious living and courtesy. *276 rooms, 201 E Franklin St., Tel. 804/788-80 00, Fax 225-03 34, category 1*

SURROUNDING AREA

Skyline Drive   (104/C1–2)

This scenic highway takes you through the Blue Ridge Mountains. Beginning near the town of *Front Royal on Interstate Hwy. 66,* it goes on south with panoramic ◆ views of the *Piedmont* to the east. Farmland bought up by the Federal government during the 1930s Depression and left fallow in the beautiful *Shenandoah Valley* is a magnificent sight. In autumn, when the leaves turn red and gold, the Skyline Drive is popular with Washington, D.C., residents, who have bought old houses in the small towns and lovingly restored them. Apple orchards and horses keep urbanites busy at weekends. During the week, the region seems deserted. Car parks (parking lots) are posted with signs leading to a network of well marked trails through the silent woods of the Blue Ridge Mountains, for instance from *Big Meadows Lodge* to *Dark Hollow Falls* and from *milemarker 45* to the peak - the climb is not an easy one – of *Old Rag Mountain* with ◆ panoramic views across most of Virginia. If you're looking for a long and arduous hike, more than 3,200 km of the famous ★ *Appalachian Trail* await you. *(Information and free permits needed for camping out in the woods available at the Visitor Centers, Tel. 703/999-22 66, on Skyline Drive 6 km south of the north feeder road and at milemarker 50).* Two mountain lodges, *Skyland Lodge* and *Big Meadows Lodge,* have hotel rooms, log cabins and restaurants right on Skyline Drive *(ARA Services, Tel. 703/743-51 08, no Fax, categories 1–3).*

The not just romantic South

*The New South at its most modern:
sunshine in America's holiday playground*

Georgia and Florida have a border in common but that's about all. The biggest of the Southern States in area, Georgia is a state of contrasts. On the one hand, its capital, Atlanta, is a city that likes to view itself as the undeclared capital of the South. Nearly half of all Georgia residents live in Atlanta. Then there's the rest of the state, much of it agrarian although Cobb County outside Atlanta is the home of important defence industries. Georgia also has a really lovely old city, Savannah, the gateway to the beautiful Sea Islands. The contrast between Savannah and Atlanta, the 1996 Summer Olympic venue, could not be sharper. Atlanta reveals no trace of the romantic ambience with which other Southern cities and towns are so richly endowed. Instead, it is a modern metropolis, a foretaste of where urban development is going in the warm climate zones. Atlanta epitomizes the *New South,* with an airport which, depending on the standards by which it is measured, handles the world's greatest volume of air traffic as a hub for domestic flights and flights to and from abroad. The global television network CNN is Atlanta-based, as is another giant, the Coca-Cola corporation. In rural Georgia, on the other hand, the agrarian economy is in terminal decline, symbolized by the hoary Spanish moss festooning huge live oaks.

Florida is something else again. Blessed with sunshine throughout the year and fabulously warm winters, Florida is America's favourite holiday spot, the playground of the rich, the poor, the old and the young. It, too, has an economy based in part on industry and commerce, and certainly the Florida citrus industry looms large. However, tourism and holidaying are what Florida is all about as far as visitors are concerned. A gently curving peninsula at the southernmost tip of the continent, Florida is not all that long and broad. Visitors often find that 14 days are enough for enjoying a holiday packed with adventure and entertainment, making

*The New South:
skyscrapers in Atlanta*

45

MARCO POLO SELECTION: GEORGIA AND FLORIDA

every day a *fun day.* Sports and Disney World, Art Déco architecture, beaches, chic shopping, entire colonies of sun-bronzed old-age pensioners and nightlife of all kinds make for a kaleidoscopic whirl of impressions and experiences that leave you with the feeling only orange juice will put you back on your feet again for some rest and relaxation. The northern part of Florida, with the port of Jacksonville, the state capital Tallahassee and the *Panhandle* jutting westward along the Gulf do not seem so holiday-oriented, perhaps because winter temperatures do fall to freezing here, albeit only rarely. South of the Daytona Beach-Cedar Key line, however, Florida is the best place in the US for lazing on the beach and soaking up tropical sun.

To learn all about this wonderland, see the MARCO POLO book on Florida.

ATLANTA

☛ City Map on page 109

(103/D5) Depending on how your plane lands in Atlanta you can see the whole city (population 2.5 million) spread out below you. A belt of suburbs with concentric rings of single-family houses has sprung up on green-field sites around the business section of the city with its skyscrapers rising up like stalagmites. In the summer of 1865 the Yankee general William Tecumseh Sherman was sweeping through Georgia on his notorious 'March to the Sea.' He began the siege of Atlanta that summer and the city surrendered in September. It burned to the ground on 16 November. Sherman was jubilant: behind his victorious armies lay Atlanta, smouldering ruins with a pall of black smoke rising high into the air and settling like a shroud over the ruined city. Military historians cite Sherman's march with the burning and pillaging it left in its wake as the first example of the modern conception of 'total war', anticipating World War II by 75 years even though Sherman's government was engaged in a just cause as far as ending slavery was concerned. The journalist Margaret Mitchell (1900-49) never knew the Atlanta she described so poignantly in her bestselling novel 'Gone with the Wind', written in 1936 and memorably filmed in 1939. Nor was she to repeat her instant worldwide success. At only 48, she was hit by a taxi and killed while she was crossing 'her' street, Peachtree Street.

The Atlanta that gave birth to the Reverend Martin Luther King, Jr., winner of the 1964 Nobel peace prize, and saw the rise of the Civil Rights movement he founded is also ambivalent. On the one hand, Maynard Jackson became the first African American to be elected mayor of a major US city in Atlanta. On the other, Black Americans are not doing any better on the whole here than in most other parts of the urban East and Middle West. Despite economic and social gains made by blacks in the years since King was assassinated in Memphis in 1968, they still represent an underclass in Atlanta.

Doc John Styth Pemberton's Atlanta, or, more precisely, Asa Candler's Atlanta, is a success story. In 1886 Dr. Pemberton invented a drink, which was at first sold as a Brain Tonic at a pharmacist's for 5 cents a glass. Candler, the owner of a pharmaceutical firm, bought out the rights to it in 1888. In 1894 it was sold for the first time in a *drugstore* in Vicksburg, Mississippi. By now it was in bottles and Coca-Cola

was set to conquer the world. Fifty years later it was no exaggeration to claim 'Atlanta is the Candlers and Coca-Cola and the Candlers and Coca-Cola are Atlanta.'

Another career launched in Atlanta, but not until the 1980s, was to span the globe. The media mogul Ted Turner started out at the bottom. From his father he inherited a firm that rented advertising space. Today his global empire is number one in media communications, at least in the news sector. 'His' CNN is received throughout the world as *real time television*. When a politician in Moscow gives a speech, he can watch himself on television. Signals are sent by satellite to Atlanta and from there across the world. Atlanta itself has hardly appeared in the news on CNN since the 1996 summer Olympics. The CNN policy is concentration on major events throughout the 'global village', which it has helped to shape, and not the city where its headquarters are located.

The American architect John Portman has also had a hand in moulding Atlanta and a highly visible one. He gave modern *downtown* Atlanta the urban feature which surprised those who went to the 1996 Olympic games. In revolutionizing hotel design, he invented the concept which has prevailed in urban planning in Atlanta, one that reflects soci-economic reality. It looks like this. Twenty – or even seventy-storey buildings are built around inner courts. Balconies and lifts like glass rockets overlook the courts. Down below, at ground floor level, giant patios are really interior plazas with restaurants and shops. Moreover, many of the skyscrapers are interlinked. In Atlanta the world is inside out. Life goes on inside these high-rise enclaves and problems like 34°C (93°F) summer weather, inadequate public transport and Old South urban and rural poverty are shut out.

SIGHTS

CNN Center
★ An ultra-modern office and hotel complex housing the CNN studios. *Daily 9 am–6 pm; 45-minute guided tours through the station rooms, always on the hour; admission US $7; Marietta St./Techwood Dr.; Tel. 404/827-23 00*

Martin Luther King Jr. Historic District
The archives, the library and the house where the black minister and Civil Rights fighter was born as well as his grave and Ebenezer Baptist Church, where he officiated during his ministry. *Daily 10 am–5 pm; admission free; Auburn Av. near Charles Allen Dr.; Tel. 404/331-39 19*

Peachtree Center
The office centre of the future, one of the most spectacular achievements of modern urban architecture with the 70-storey (a world record) *Westin Hotel,* a luxury mall and inside gardens. *Daily; admission free; on the block formed by Baker, Ellis, Williams and Courtland Sts.*

Underground Atlanta
Beneath the streets of the modern city is a labyrinth of cobble-stone alleys and buildings, the only ones to have survived the great fire of 1865. During the siege of Atlanta the whole area was a gigantic field hospital. Since the area was restored and reopened in 1989, it has been a Town Center with art exhibitions, restaurants, night clubs and street artists. *Daily; admission free; Alabama St./Central Av.; Tel. 404/523-23 11*

MUSEUM

The World of Coca-Cola Pavilion
When H. L. Mencken described the South in the New York Evening Mail on 13 November 1917 as a Sahara of the Bozart *beaux-arts* written as a Southerner would have pronounced it, he was besieged with letters from enraged readers: 'Who has not heard of Asa G. Candler, whose name is synonymous with Coca-Cola, a Georgia product?' *Well now,* this is where you can study a great cultural achievement, a century of Coke. *Mon–Sat 10 am–8.30 pm, Sun noon–5 pm; admission US $6; next to Underground Atlanta, Martin Luther King Jr. Dr./Central Av.; Tel. 404/676-51 51*

RESTAURANTS

Like everything else that's interesting in Atlanta, they are inside malls and hotels and not open to view. There isn't much real Southern cooking. You'll find mainly international and ethnic cuisine.

Dining Room
Chef Günther Seeger earned two Michelin stars in the German Black Forest before coming here to preside over Atlanta haute cuisine. His menus are innovative and change constantly. The wine list is superb. *Mon–Fri lunch and dinner, Sat dinner only,*

Sun and holidays closed; Ritz-Carlton Buckhead Hotel, 3434 Peachtree Rd. NE, Tel. 404/237-27 00, category 1

103 West

If prizes were awarded for kitsch, the popular restaurant 103 West would probably have been among the winners. American and French cuisine is delicious in a setting of simulated marble and trompe-l'oeil. *Mon–Sat 6 pm– 11 pm, 103 W Paces Ferry Rd., Tel. 404/233-59 93, category 1*

Sierra Grill

Oysters with red-hot sauce, fajitas, trout and chiles relleños – done the way you love them in the Sierras of New Mexico. *Mon–Fri 11 am–3 pm and 5.30 pm–10 pm, Sat 5.30 pm–11 pm, 1529 Piedmont Rd., Tel. 404/873-53 60, category 3*

SHOPPING

Lenox Square/Phipps Plaza

✪ One of the biggest malls in the US with turnover to match. Whatever you'd find in the big New York department stores and jewellers, you can buy from their branches here: Macy's, Saks, Tiffany and dozens of other boutiques and elegant department stores. *Daily 9 am– 9 pm, opening hours vary from store to store, Peachtree Rd./Lenox Rd.*

HOTELS

Downtown it is impossible to find cheap hotel rooms. If you can only afford less than US $100 a night, you'll have to find something on the outskirts of the city.

Ansley Inn

Bed & Breakfast in English-inspired stockbroker's Tudor in Midtown, one of the prettiest and earliest of Atlanta's attractive residential sections. Rooms furnished in reproductions of 18th-century antiques. *12 rooms, 253 15th St., Tel. 404/872-90 00, Fax 892-23 18, categories 1–2*

Motel 6 West

Comfortable at unbeatable prices but 25 mins. drive from the centre of town. Pool. *175 rooms, 4100 Wendell Dr. SW, Tel. 404/696-07 57, Fax 696-52 62, category 3*

Omni

Straight out of science fiction: from your balcony you'll look straight into the CNN studios and 15 storeys of high-tech facade. Cosy? No. Interesting? Yes. *471 rooms, 100 CNN Center, Tel. 404/659-00 00, Fax 525-50 50, category 1*

Westin Peachtree Plaza

Try to book a room on the 70th floor: this is the world's tallest hotel. It offers all the luxury in the world, too. Despite its size, this hostelry is known for astonishingly friendly service. A remarkable enclosed court with waterfalls splashing 8 storeys. *1080 rooms, 210 Peachtree St., Tel. 404/659-14 00, Fax 589-74 24, category 1*

INFORMATION

Visitor Information Center

Mon–Fri 9 am–6 pm, Peachtree Center Mall, Tel. 404/521-66 33 and 329-45 00 (taped updates on events calendar), Fax 521-65 62

Stone Mountain (103/D5)
A monumental relief has been carved into the face of a sheer monolith about 25 km east of Atlanta on US 78. It depicts equestrian Confederate heroes, President Jefferson Davis and the generals Robert E. Lee and Stonewall Jackson. Around the granite rock, which is at least 1 km in circumference, cluster amusement and theme parks, among them the *Stone Mountain Railroad,* a *Paddlewheel Riverboat,* an *Antebellum Plantation,* an *Automobile Museum* and a little *zoo.*

For those unable or unwilling to ascend the rock, a cable-car runs past the relief, which measures 30 x 63 m. At the foot of the rock there is a lake with beaches for swimming and sunbathing. In the evenings *son et lumière* with laser beams. *Daily 6 am–midnight; admission US $6 a car, extra charge for attractions; US 78, Stone Mountain; Tel. 404/498-56 00*

DAYTONA BEACH

(107/E3) ☈ *Spring Break* is the short break US college students have in the spring between semesters or trimesters. During that time,

The Old South: Civil War heroes at Stone Mountain

thousands of students from East Coast universities and colleges head like lemmings to Florida, and Daytona Beach is one of their favourite haunts. Sprawling endlessly along the coast, the city consists mainly of motels, fast-food joints and shops selling bathing and beach gear. Because the sand is so firm, cars are permitted to drive along the 40 km of beach. During the day students flaunt their muscles and curves. By afternoon the whole show boils down to exciting contests like Who can belly flop the loudest?, Who's wearing the littlest bikini? and Who's got the most beautiful pectorals in a wet T-shirt?. In the evening everyone goes to parties, beach and otherwise, and discos.

RESTAURANT

Down the Hatch
A seafood restaurant, which differs markedly from the usual Daytona Beach fast-food eateries by offering an incredible *all you can eat* seafood buffet groaning with oysters, shrimp, crab and sea bass. *Daily 11.30 am–10 pm, 4984 Front St., Tel. 904/761-48 31, category 3*

HOTELS

During the car racing season in Feburary, March and June as well as during the college and university Spring Break period, hotels here are usually booked up. At any rate prices are higher and you have to stay at least 3 to 5 days.

Captain's Quarters Inn
A family inn at the quiet southern end of town with large, cosy rooms with Colonial style décor.

Seaview balconies, heated pool. *19 rooms, 3711 S Atlantic Av., Tel. 904/767-31 19, Fax 767-08 83, category 2*

Howard Johnson Plaza
The number one party hotel in the Party District on the boardwalk. There's an Olympic-sized pool, a disco and the site of all the Miss contests. Daily pool party and lots of other fun things to do. *334 rooms, 600 N Atlantic Av., Tel. 904/258-85 22, Fax 257-91 27, categories 1–2*

ENTERTAINMENT

Ocean Deck
⚑ Bar with live Reggae music every evening. *Daily noon–midnight, 127 S Ocean Av., Tel. 904/253-52 24*

Razzle's
Currently the in place to go, a ⚑ giant disco with an Ultra-Light show and competitions every evening like the popular *Wet T-Shirt Contest. Daily 7 pm–3 am, 611 Seabreeze Bd., Tel. 904/257-62 36*

INFORMATION

Destination Daytona
Mon–Fri 9 am–5 pm, 126 E Orange Av., P.O. Box 910, Daytona Beach, FL 32115, Tel. 904/255-04 15, Fax 255-54 78

FORT LAUDERDALE

(107/E–F5) 'Florida's Venice' doesn't have all that much in common with the Italian pearl of the lagoon although you can dash about the broad waterways in water taxis, which are tremendous fun. Fort Lauderdale is, together with Miami and several cities to the north, part of a conurbation stretching along the southeastern Atlantic coast. It has become a winter holiday venue for sun-worshippers from all over the world. This is a particularly popular spot with Americans who can afford to stay here and keep up holiday homes or winter and retirement residences built to accommodate two big cars in front and a yacht in back. That's why visitors love to gaze at 'Millionaires' Row', where the houses are especially grand and the yachts notably large. Fort Lauderdale does have one major drawback for visitors from abroad: many of the beach hotels are cut off from the beach by Atlantic Avenue, a broad thoroughfare. Some large hotels do have their own yacht marinas, perfect for Americans sailing up and down the Intracoastal Waterway along the Florida east coast, but these hotels are far from the beach.

SIGHTS

Jungle Queen
Sightseeing by pleasure craft, cruising past Millionaires' Row, *downtown Fort Lauderdale,* a Seminole Indian village, the big yacht marinas – all from the water. *Departures daily 10 am and 2 pm, takes 3 hours; tickets cost US $10.95, a Dinner Cruise, daily at 7 pm, takes 4 hours, US $23,95, at Bahia Mar Yacht Center, S Ocean Bd., not too far south of Las Olas Bd., Tel. 954/462-55 96*

RESTAURANT

15th Street Fisheries
Amid nets and lobster pots as if you were on a fishing boat. Mar-

vellous fresh seafood but steaks and other classics are on the menu. *Daily from 5 pm, booking essential, 1900 SE 15th St., Tel. 954/763-27 77, categories 2–3*

SHOPPING

The Galleria
A mall with branches of the New York department stores Saks Fifth Avenue and Brooks Brothers (owned by Marks & Spencer) as well as about 150 other shops. About 1 km from the beach. *Mon–Fri 10 am–9 pm, Sat 10 am–6 pm, Sun 12.30 pm– 5.30 pm, E Sunrise Bd. between A1A and Federal Hwy.*

HOTELS

Bahia Cabana Beach Resort
A motel consisting of several buildings on the Intracoastal Waterway. The rustic restaurant with a bar and live music every evening is popular with ✪ the locals. However, it does make this part of the motel rather noisy. *116 rooms, 3001 Harbor Dr., Tel. 954/524-15 55, Fax 764-59 51, category 2*

Pelican Beach Resort
The city's most attractive little motel and one of very few places to stay directly on the beach, with sunny rooms decorated in the Mediterranean style. A small pool. Breakfast included in the price. *77 rooms, 2000 N Atlantic Bd., Tel. 954/568-94 31, Fax 565-26 22, categories 1–2*

SPORTS & LEISURE

Ocean Watersports
Kayaking, windsurfing, sailing boats – rentals and lessons. *Kayaks*

Florida sights: the Fort Lauderdale yacht marina

US $10 an hour, surfboards US $20 an hour, on the beach about 3 blocks south of Las Olas Bd., Tel. 954/ 763-4020

ENTERTAINMENT

Mai-Kai

A Polynesian Revue and a California Chinese dinner. *Shows: Mon–Fri 7.15 pm and 10 pm, Sat and Sun 7.30 pm and 10.30 pm; admission charge US $10, meals from US $16, 3599 N Federal Hwy., Tel. 954/563-3272*

Mombasa Bay

Bar, Restaurant and disco with live music on the Intracoastal Waterway. *Mon–Sat 11.30 am–2 am, Sun 11 am–3 am, Music from 7 pm, Tues-Thurs Rhythm and Blues, Fri–Mon Reggae, admission free, 3051 NE 32nd Av., Tel. 954/565-7441*

WATER TAXIS

Water taxis are the best way to get around Fort Lauderdale in the evening. The yellow and green gondolas pick up guests as they go to hotels, shops and restaurants along the Intracoastal Waterway. *Tel. 954/467-6677 or simply pick up one of those red telephones or ask at the desk: US $5 one way, US $13 for an all-day ticket*

INFORMATION

Greater Fort Lauderdale Convention & Visitors Bureau

Mon–Fri 9 am–5 pm, 200 E Las Olas Bd., Suite 1500, Fort Lauderdale, FL 33301, Tel. 954/765-4466, Fax 765-4467

SURROUNDING AREA

Palm Beach (107/F5)

Palm Beach, an enclave of multi-millionaires (don't confuse it with West Palm Beach, the popular seaside resort) is just north of Fort Lauderdale. Non-residents are not welcome here. Forbidding walls and hedges screen off the Florida retreats of the Kennedy family *(on N Country Rd.)* and Donald Trump, the building speculator *(on S Ocean Bd.).*

KEY WEST

(107/D6) Accessible by bridge, the last bead on the string of pearls at the southernmost tip of the US is the most beautiful. Ernest Hemingway spent quite a few years here when he no longer went to Africa or could live in Cuba. It's worth the five-hour drive from Miami – the last section of it on the Overseas Hwy. which links the 28 islands. You can see why Papa felt at home here. This must be one of the craziest places, with the possible exception of Hawaii, in the United States. Lovely conch houses made of wood by mariners who modelled them on whatever caught their fancy in the world's ports; palm groves; the Gulf of Mexico, a magnet for fishermen and treasure hunters (so many Spanish galleons went down here), full of coral reefs. Outsiders and insiders are welcome in Key West, where Hemingway look-alikes jostle for the limelight.

SIGHTS

Ernest Hemingway Home and Museum
★ Hemingway lived here with his last wife and worked in a building separate from the Spanish colonial-style house, which was built in 1851. *Daily 9 am–5 pm; admission US $6.50; 907 Whitehead St.; Tel. 305/294-15 75*

RESTAURANT

Half Shell Raw Bar
Crab fishermen used to dock where raw oysters and mussels (hence Raw Bar) are served on the half shell. *Daily 11 am–11 pm, 920 Caroline St., Tel. 305/294-74 96, category 3*

HOTELS

Marriott's Casa Marina Resort
A historic building sumptuously restored with all modern amenities on one of the few beaches in Key West. *242 rooms, 1500 Reynolds St., Tel. 305/296-35 35, Fax 296-99 60, category 1*

Pier House
A grand old hotel, also with its own beach, featuring individually decorated rooms, a restaurant and a wine bar. *142 rooms, 1 Duval St., Tel. 305/296-46 00, Fax 296-75 69, category 1*

Southernmost Motel
A pleasant place to stay with a small pool at the southernmost tip of the US. Rooms have southern exposure facing the Gulf. *127 rooms, 1377 Duval St., Tel. 305/296-65 77, Fax 294-82 72, category 2*

ENTERTAINMENT

Captain Tony's and Sloppy Joe's
⚡ Two bars which don't wait for the evening to open, rivals in claiming the honour of having been Hemingway's favourite. Both are full of 'Papa' Hemingway memorabilia. Each claims that he loved to spin seamen's yarns there when he'd had enough to drink. After other drinks Hemingway apparently liked – some say the Cuban daiquiri others maintain it was the Cuba libre (rum and coke) and younger aficionados assert it was the margarita - it doesn't really matter which of these great bars – hic! – was the one Hemingway really frequented. *Daily 11 am until late at night; Captain Tony's Saloon: 428 Green St.; Sloppy Joe's: 201 Duval St.*

INFORMATION

Key West Chamber of Commerce
Mallory Square, 402 Wall St., Key West, FL 33040, Tel. 305/294-25 87 or 800/527-85 39

MIAMI

(107/E5) Florida's capital of glitz: something to rave about without embarrassment. When the sun sets in the Gulf of Mexico and the sky goes lavender, its long last rays tinge the glass skyscrapers with gold and orange and the pelicans drop – plop – from the landing stages into the Atlantic for one last catch, Miami wakes up and makes ready for long nights of fun.

Not with glasses of freshly squeezed o.j. *(real Florida orange juice on ice)* and not to listen to the rustle of palm fronds or even the murmur of the sea. Now it's time for indoor night-life to take over. In the Art Déco hotels of Miami Beach, models (fashion photos all seem to be taken here) freshen up their make-up. More mature members of their sex hasten to the *beauty parlors* in the vast hotels. Waiters in Cuban restaurants write up the evening's list of Tapas y Mariscos, Spanish snacks, hors d'oeuvres, consisting mainly of shellfish. Masculine members of the jeunesse dorée are already propping up the neon bars and staring expectantly into their first frozen margaritas. And, backstage, Honky Tonk women are snapping the straps of their rhinestone bras and shrugging their shoulders for a comfortable fit because, after all, this is where all those dollar bills will go later on in the evening when all else has been revealed and the strip show is still fresh in the minds of well-heeled customers in search of vicarious sex.

SIGHTS

Art Déco District of Miami Beach

★ Chalky pink and other pastel shades, porthole windows from the great era of the transatlantic liner and ocean-going motor yachts and wavy eyebrows above the windows: throughout southern Miami beach delicate tints and nautical touches. Built in the roaring Twenties and the 1930s, this section of the city represents the world's largest cluster of Art Déco domestic architecture. Not all that long ago this glorious monument to the Moderns was threatened by demolition. The

Saved from the wreckers: Art Déco in Miami Beach

ravages of time and salty breezes off the Atlantic had left facades crumbling. The only people still teetering on rickety aluminium chairs in front of the hotels were senior citizens making their meagre pensions go a long way. Building speculators were ravenous for a new Miami Beach. However, concerned residents fought them off and the 40 blocks of this district were entered in the National Register of Historic Places. Fashion photographers developed a foible for sloe-eyed beauties posed against a backdrop of garish 1950s Cadillacs and austere geometry.

Guided tours take 1 1/2 hours (on foot) through the Art Déco section put on by the Miami Design Preservation League: *Sat 10.30 am; US $6; Sun 10.30 am bicycle tour; US $10; 1244 Ocean Dr.; Tel. 305/672-20 14*

Bayside Marketplace

★ Strictly speaking, Bayside Marketplace should be mentioned under the heading of 'shopping rather than sightseeing'. However, the justification for touching on it here instead is based on compelling sociological arguments. Shopping is a way of life for many US citizens and Bayside epitomizes shopping although this isn't a mall in the conventional sense of the word. Most malls are bulky concrete blocks whose marvels are only revealed from the inside. No, Bayside Market place consists of two open, curvilinear pavilions on the yacht marina. Urban planners have tried to emulate the classical covered market with overtones of the Oriental bazaar. Consequently, here you'll find small kiosks and booths as well as snack bars serving ethnic food from across the world, jugglers, parrots and musicians instead of department store branches. Bayside represents a deliberate return to an age-old institution which has been rediscovered in the US. *Daily 10 am–10 pm, 401 Biscayne Bd., Miami*

Downtown towers

There wasn't much space to build in downtown Miami but the money was there, lots of it, laundered so many times that it was as pastel as the houses. The answer was to hire the best architects and give them a free hand to build glass skyscrapers. The tints of the changing sky reflected on them conceals the fact that a third of the modern office space in these post-modern towers is empty. Yet another modern achievement here suffers from neglect: the Metro Mover, an ultra-modern elevated railway encircling the city centre and affording views of it from huge windows. The ideal way to sightsee: tickets cost a mere 25 cents.

Vizcaya

Let's go back into the past to 1916. James Deering had made a fortune in mowing hay. The company he founded, International Harvester, threw up such comfortable profit margins that he was able to spend US $15 million, in those days an unbelievable sum, on building a villa in South Miami. That was enough to finance an eclectic blend of Rococo, Baroque, Renaissance and Neo-Classicism set in stringently laid-out gardens. The Deering palace on Biscayne Bay boasts 70 rooms full of art treasures from all over the world. Deering even had enough money left over to moor a stone launch in front of it to serve as a breakwater, a good investment in the future. During Prohibition boats landed here. No one knows for sure but it certainly seems possible that rum runners and whisky smugglers who came across from Cuba and the Caribbean islands may have docked here, engaged in one of the most, if not *the* most, lucrative trades of the era. *Daily 9.30 am–4.30 pm; admission US $10; 3251 S Miami Av.; Tel. 305/250-91 33*

RESTAURANTS

Joe's Seafood Market
Superb American seafood: shrimp, lobster, sea bass, pompano etc at incredibly reasonable prices for top quality. *Daily 11 am–10 pm; 400 NW North River Dr. (hard to find since it's right on a pier: Biscayne Bd. to NW 3rd St., and stay with it until you turn right into North River Dr.); Tel. 305/374-56 37, category 2*

Versailles
Cubans eat here. A Hall of Mirrors like Versailles. The medianoche sandwiches are even more of an unexpected treat. Cuban cuisine in Little Havana. *Mon–Sat 8 am– 2 am, Sun 9 am–2 am, 3555 SW 8th St., Tel. 305/444-02 40, category 2*

HOTELS

On *Ocean Drive* in *Miami Beach* there are some Art Déco hotels in the medium price range. Further north on *Collins Avenue* you can't miss the big hotels and the motels are north of these.

Cardozo
The ultimate in restored Art Déco, this Miami Beach hotel is on the beach. Not all the rooms boast period furniture. If you want the best on offer here, just ask for *a renovated ocean view room, please. 49 rooms, 1144 Ocean Dr., Miami Beach, Tel. 305/534-21 35, Fax 531-55 43, category 1. A 30 per cent summer discount*

Fontainebleau Hilton Resort and Spa
Although this is part of the chain, it's in the top segment of it: a tropical poolscape, right on the beach, sport facilities, beauty and hairdressing salons, elegant restaurants. *1266 rooms, 4441 Collins Av., Miami Beach, Tel. 305/538-2000, Fax 674-46 07, category 1. A 25 per cent summer discount*

The New Waterside Inn
A basic motel. Pool, conveniently near the beach. *90 rooms, 2360 Collins Av., Miami Beach, Tel. 305/538-19 51, Fax 531-32 17, category 3*

SPORTS & LEISURE

Surfboard rentals on the beach at *Miami Beach* and on *Rickenbacker Causeway* to *Key Biscayne* (for beginners). Tennis, golf, deep-sea fishing: ask at your hotel.

ENTERTAINMENT

Clevelander Poolside Bar
⚡ An open-air neon bar made of glass brick where everybody meets. *Daily noon–4 am, 1020 Ocean Dr., Miami Beach, Tel. 305/531-34 85*

Club Tropigala
A high energy revue, dancers with endlessly long legs. *Wed–Sun 7 pm*

to dawn, admission US$13.50, for Dinner Show US$39, in the Hilton Hotel, 4441 Collins Av., Tel. 305/538-2000

Penrod's on the Beach
🕺 Disco and a bar that's a great place for meeting people. Beach and pool. Young people hang out here. *Sun–Thurs 11 pm–2 am, Fri, Sat 11 pm–5 am, Miami Beach, Ocean Dr./ 1st St., Tel. 305/538-11 11*

Greater Miami
Convention and Visitor Bureau
701 Brickell Av., Miami, Suite 2700, Tel. 305/539-3000, Fax 539-31 13, Mon–Fri 9 am–6 pm

Everglades   (107/E5–6)
The world-famous tropical swamps, the largest wetlands in North America, full of rare animals, birds, plants and trees, is just west of the outskirts of Miami. Basically this is a silted-up river oozing south, 80 km across and only a few centimetres deep in places. *Main way into the national park on State Road 9336 near Florida City (from Hwy. US 1); admission US $10 a car; other entrances in Shark Valley and at Everglades City (from US Hwy. 41)*

ORLANDO

(107/E3) The home of Mickey and Minnie. Without Disney, this would just be a sleepy central Florida retirement community. Thanks to the various Disneylands as well as a dozen other theme and amusement parks, Orlando is a growing, booming and lively city. *Universal Studios* had the master of illusion, Steven Spielberg, build a park to rival the achievement of *Disney-MGM Studios*. At *Sea World*, a killer whale named Shamu, weighing 2,000 kg, kisses his lovely attendants. If you want to play in the water without fear of jellyfish, give *Wet 'n' Wild* a try, Orlando's substitute for beach life: kamikazi slides and a surfpool with giant waves; or you can banquet with Henry VIII in medieval paper machée castles or be locked up in a dungeon just for fun. Orlando, a sprawling and amorphous city, is a wildly successful animated cartoon.

Universal Studios Florida
Major contributions to world entertainment cinema like King Kong, E.T. or Back to the Future – this is where you can be part of them. On the Earthquake Ride you'll survive a quake registering 8.3 points on the Richter Scale. You can saunter down Sunset Boulevard in Hollywood, walk through New York's Central Park or around San Francisco's Ghirardelli Square – why even bother to go anywhere else? *Daily 9 am–11 pm; adults US $39.75, children aged 3 to 9 US $32, 3 and younger free; 1000 Universal Studios Plaza, Exit 30 West on Interstate Hwy. 14, near the intersection of Hwy. 14 and the Florida Turnpike; Tel. 407/363-8000*

Walt Disney World
★ Ready for more? Then on to *Disney-MGM Studios* with Aliens, Indiana Jones and *Grauman's*

Chinese Theater, all of this only a minuscule corner of Disney World. The *Magic Kingdom* with *Cinderella's Castle* and good old *Main Street USA* is for Disney purists, who know them from Los Angeles and Paris. The *EPCOT Center* (Experimental Prototype Community of Tomorrow) shows you exactly how Americans imagined the future a decade ago. With hindsight, this residential community has its charms. But the three main parks are not all there is to Disney World. There are waterworlds and adventure worlds like *Discovery Island, River Country* and *Typhoon Lagoon*. It's utterly impossible to take in more than one park a day and, don't forget, parks like the Magic Kingdom are so popular that you'll queue up for 1 to 1 1/2 hours to get into each one of the attractions.

Walt Disney World is, legally speaking, a separate community. *Daily 9 am till at least 8 pm, most parts 11 pm or midnight; Tickets for a whole day for one park: adults US $39.75, children aged 3 to 9 US $32,* *3 and under free, 4-day pass for all three big parks: US $150 and US $120; 5-day pass for the parks plus Pleasure Island, Typhoon Lagoon, River Country and Discovery Island: US$205 and US $164; access via I 4 or Irlo Bronson Memorial Hwy. (192/530); parts of the parks are clearly sign-posted; Tel. 407/824-8000 (for booking tickets in advance), 407/824-43 21 (Information), 407/824-4500 (Guest Relations – all the help you need)*

HOTELS

Disney World has hotels in all categories and even a superb camping site for visitors with tents. *Tel. 407/824-8000*

SURROUNDING AREA

John F. Kennedy (107/E3) Space Center

Less than an hour's drive east of Orlando lies *Cape Canaveral,* where space-shuttle missions take off into space and sometimes land. Bus tours through the base start at the *Visitor Center,* bristling

Pointing to yesterday's future: rockets at the Space Center

with rockets, space capsules and a space shuttle fitted with its boosters. They take you to the *Observation Gantry,* the tower where important visitors watch launches, to the *Apollo/Saturn V Center,* which dates from the era of Moon Landings, to the *International Space Station Center,* where the International Space Station (ISS) is now being built can be viewed, the *Space Shuttle Launch Pads,* where the rockets take off, to the gigantic *Vehicle Assembly Building,* where space shuttles are mounted on rockets, and to a host of other space facilities. You can linger at any one attraction as long as you like and catch the next bus to move on. *Daily 9.45 am to 2 hours before sunset, bus departure times depend on the number of visitors. When launches are going on, tour schedules are changed or tours may be cancelled altogether.*

Imax cinemas at the Visitor Center show exciting films on space travel. The *Mission Pass for the Space Center Tour includes two Imax films US $26, children aged 3 to 11 US $20, Crew Pass for the Space Center Tour and one Imax film US $19, children US $15, Kennedy Space Center, Spaceport USA, Tel. 407/452-21 21*

SAINT AUGUSTINE

(**107/E2**) In 1513 the Spanish Conquistador Ponce de León went ashore in northern Florida, as legend has it, in search of the Fountain of Youth but more likely looking for gold. Saint Augustine is proud of being the oldest city in the US. For a long time the city was a Spanish Colony, with cyclopean massive *Castillo San Marcos,* which has walls

10 m thick and 5 m high, its impregnable stronghold.

SIGHTS

Castillo de San Marcos
The massive Spanish fortress, which was never taken by foes. *Daily 8.45 am–4.45 pm; admission US $4, minors up to 17 free; 1 Castillo Dr.*

Historic District
The most entertaining way to view the Historic District is to be driven through it in a one- or two-horse carriage. The coachmen's history lessons are probably more fantasy than fact. *Colee's Sightseeing Carriage Tours, daily 8.30 am–5 pm, in summer till midnight, prices depend on carriage size and tour duration: from US $35 an hour, leav-ing from Bayfront near Castillo de San Marcos, Tel. 904/829-28 18*

RESTAURANTS

Café Camacho
An elegant Cuban café and restaurant. Café con leche is a welcome alternative to the weak coffee served at US diners and breakfast joints. Cuban sandwiches at noon and in the evening *boliche* (roast meat served with black-eyed beans and rice). *Daily 9 am–9 pm, 11-C Avilles St., Tel. 904/824-70 30, category 3*

Santa Maria Restaurant
An old dry dock on Saint Augustine Bay with a view of the old Bridge of Lions. Specialities: Balearic fish de maestrez, shrimp, Florida lobster. *In Summer daily except Wed noon–10 pm, in winter Fri–Mon noon–10 pm, Tues–Thurs 5 pm–10 pm, 135 Av. Menendez, Tel. 904/829-65 78, category 2*

The Old Town is surrounded by motels and hotels in all price ranges. As elsewhere in the South, Bed & Breakfasts are the place to stay, especially here in the Historic Quarter. Remember, smoking is prohibited in these old wooden buildings as at nearly all B & Bs throughout the US.

Casa de Solona
Built in 1763 and furnished with antiques. Breakfast, evening sherry and bicycles included in the price. *4 suites, 21 Aviles St., Tel. 904/824-35 55, Fax 824-33 16, category 1*

Westcott House
An 1880s Southern mansion with beautiful, welcoming porches and American period furniture. *8 rooms, 146 Av. Menendez, Tel. and Fax 904/824-43 01, category 1*

St. Augustine and St. Johns County Visitor Information and Preview Center
10 Castillo Dr., Saint Augustine, FL 32084, Tel. 904/825-10 00, E-Mail: tdc@co.st-johns.fl.us

SAVANNAH

(103/F6) Muggy summers here feature the Old South at its sleepiest. History has been fickle to this lovely city on the Georgia coast. Laid out on the 18th-century grid plan in 1773, it was the last major British effort at urban planning in America before the colonies revolted. On his March to the Sea General Sherman didn't do much to

Savannah because it had already been evacuated by the time he reached it. Before the Civil War, it shared the honours with Charleston, SC, as the Southeastern seaboard's major cotton port. After the war Savannah went into a long decline without slaves to work the plantations that produced the silky, long-staple Sea Island cotton off shore. Long after Sea Island cotton was again on the world market, Savannah residents began to restore the city, which, oddly enough, is scarcely mentioned in the standard American travel guides. A walk through this venerable city with its mossy live oaks takes you to the heart of what has remained of the Old South. The *Historic District* is at the centre of the grid. No two houses are alike. Even more than Charleston and New Orleans, Savannah has retained its Southern character. Columned porches, superb facades, wrought-iron balconies, dusty pastel colours and live oaks, camellias – in winter – and pines. Untouched by war, trends and tourism, Savannah is the authentic South and not an historical theme parc.

General James Oglethorpe had Savannah laid out on a grid plan with plenty of space allotted to gardens and squares (24 in all) as well as residential areas. This is one of the few US cities that is really enjoyable to explore on foot. However, the mean July temperature is 27°C (81°F). Moreover, between July and September you may be caught

Where Freemasons were finally free: Freemasons' Hall, Savannah

in a tropical downpour and drenched through without warning. Old trees shade the streets. *The historic buildings that are open to the public can usually be visited on the days listed below between 9 am and 5 pm.*

Historic houses and churches

★ Your extended walk might start at *King-Tisdell Cottage,* at *14 Hantingdon St.* just outside the historic centre, which is bounded to the south by *Gaston St.* The cottage is gingerbready, with squiggly barge boards (1896) and all the other Victorian Gothic trimmings. It houses a *Museum of Afro-American History (open daily).* Two blocks to the north you can turn west off *Gordon St.* to reach the *Mikve Israel Synagogue,* at *20 E Gordon St.,* built in 1878 by German and Portuguese Jews in the Neo-Gothic style *(Mon–Fri).* After crossing *Monterey Square* – surrounded by beautiful houses – you go on to the main north-south thoroughfare bisecting the

grid, *Ball St.,* and on up to *Madison Square* to reach *St. John's Episcopal Church,* which dates from 1840, and the *Green-Medrim House,* a Neo-Gothic mansion with a wrought-iron gate, the house General William Tecumseh Sherman requisitioned as his headquarters *(Mon–Sat).* Then continue on north up *Bull St.* to *Chippewa Square* with the *First Baptist Church,* the oldest church of this denomination in Georgia, on to the *Barrow Mansion,* now used by an insurance company, and the oldest theatre still used for its original purpose in the US, the *Savannah Theatre.* At the *corner of Bull St.* and *Oglethorpe Av.* stands a house built in 1821 in the Regency-style (1810–20 and in country towns up to 1835 in Britain), the *birthplace* of the woman who founded the Girl Scouts of America, Juliette Gordon Low. In *State St.* you pass the *Lutheran Church of the Ascension* on your right as you head for the *Owens-Thomas House* at *124 Abercorn St.,*

62

built in 1816 and regarded as the finest Regency house in the US *(daily except for Sept)*. Not far south of it on *State St.*, at *324 E State St.*, you'll see *Davenport House*, built in 1820 in the Georgia Federal style with superb antiques and an ellipsoid stair *(daily)*. Go north on any street to *St. Julian St.*, then continue on it westward across *Warren Square* and *Reynolds Square* to *Johnson Square*, and *Christ Episcopal Church (Tues–Fri)*, with Neo-Classical white columns. It dates from 1838 and stands on the site of the first church built by settlers here, in 1733. Just north of *Johnson Square*, at the end of *Bull St.*, stands *City Hall*, a Neo-Classical building sporting the copper-clad dome typical of late 19th-century US public buildings.

The whole *Historic District* covers an area of only about 2 x 3 km. It will take you several days to see what's inside the buildings here.

RESTAURANTS

Elisabeth on 37th

Run by a couple with exquisite taste – she cooks and he is a lawyer, antiques collector and wine connoisseur – this is Savannah's best restaurant. Southern cooking at its finest and that is saying a lot. Try Shrimp Savannah or beautifully seasoned quail or mushroom pancakes. *105 E 37th St., Tel. 912/236-55 47, Mon–Sat dinner, closed Sun, religious holidays and in Aug, categories 1–2*

Il Pasticcio

Looks like the Old Country: a lovely Art Déco restaurant and art gallery. The menu varies constantly, featuring northern Italian specialities, superb wines. Right at the centre of town. *2 E Broughton, Tel. 912/231-88 88, daily, dinner, categories 1–2*

HOTELS

Foley House

Bed & Breakfast in two lovely old Savannah town houses in the Historic District, restored and sumptuously furnished with antiques and old china. Extraordinary service and utter luxury, eg jacuzzis with some rooms, *19 rooms, 14 W Hull St., Tel. 912/232-66 22, Fax 231-12 18, category 1*

Forsyth Park Inn

Bed & Breakfast in a Victorian mansion with magnificently lofty – 5 m – ceilings and beautifully decorated and furnished rooms. *9 rooms and 1 separate cottage, which sleeps 4, 102 W Hall St., Tel. 912/233-68 00, no Fax, categories 1–2*

Travelodge

A good basic motel with a pool near the Historic District. *56 rooms, 512 W Oglethorpe Av., Tel. 912/233-92 51, no Fax, category 3*

ENTERTAINMENT

Waterfront Area

♀ Lots and lots of bars, restaurants and nightclubs in restored brick warehouses. *John P. Rousakis Riverfront Plaza*

INFORMATION

Savannah Visitors Bureau

Mon–Fri 8.30am–5pm, Sat, Sun 9am–5pm, 222 W Oglethorpe Av., Tel. 912/ 944-04 56, Fax 944-04 68, www. savcvb.com

Black earth and big dams

The Deep South is a land of extremes

This is the *Deep South,* a land of technical progress with poverty that has persisted longer than elsewhere in the South. According to the 1990 US census, African Americans make up about one fourth of the population of Alabama and thirty-six per cent of Mississippi's, the largest proportion of African Americans in any US state. In the *Deep South,* comprising Alabama, Mississippi and Louisiana, discriminatory Jim Crow laws lasted here longer than in the rest of the South. Segregation in schools has slowly broken down. Still it was in Montgomery, Alabama, that a black woman's arrest for refusing to sit in the back rows of a segregated bus in 1955 led to the beginning of the Civil Rights movement. A year later the Supreme Court struck down Alabama laws enforcing segregation on buses as unconstitutional. Freedom Rides started in Alabama, too – at Anniston. The term used for part of this region, *Black Belt,* is not, however, a racist slur. On the contrary,

The pride of the New South: the moon landing capsule

it stands for the strip of sticky but black clay soil that links the two states of Alabama and Mississippi from Montgomery to the Mississippi River.

It seems easy to distinguish the Deep South states geographically although they boast only one common distinctive scenic feature: inland waterways and dams. The state borders were drawn long and straight. The long Appalachian Mountain System ends in Alabama. In Franklin Roosevelt's administration (1933-45), the *Tennessee Valley Authority,* the first publicly owned electricity board in the US, was created by the Tennessee Valley Act as part of the 1930s' New Deal to revive the Southern economy, moribund after the crash of 1929, by generating both cheap electricity and jobs. In the *Black Belt,* where King Cotton reigned when it was covered with vast plantations worked by slave labour, huge herds of cattle now graze. To the south, along the Gulf of Mexico, the region includes the Florida *Panhandle,* thrust like a dagger into Alabama almost to Mobile. Completed in 1985, the 234-mile Tennessee-Tombigbee Waterway runs from

MARCO POLO SELECTION: ALABAMA AND MISSISSIPPI

1 Alabama Space and Rocket Center
Original NASA rockets and replica Space Shuttles (page 68)

2 The Briars
Bed & Breakfast in the house of Jefferson Davis' wife (page 70)

3 Natchez
A town on the Mississippi where time stood still after the Civil War (page 69)

4 West Ship Island
A deserted island off the Mississippi coast (page 67)

Mississippi to Alabama, vertically linking the Mississippi and Tennessee Rivers. Visitors flock to the southern part of this region, attracted by the cosmopolitan city of New Orleans or the powdery, nearly white sandy beach stretching as far as the Alabama *Gulf Coast Delta,* much of it man-made like the Tenn-Tom. The 40 km of sand south of US Hwy. 90 may be the world's longest man-made beach. In the flat hinterland to the north, summers are notorious for heat, humidity and mosquitoes.

BILOXI

(**101/E5**) This attractive city, once the capital of French Louisiana, occupies a narrow peninsula on the long man-made beach in Mississippi mentioned above. By the late 17th century, Biloxi was popular with Mississippi plantation owners. It still has a lot of that sleepy Southern charm, especially in the *Vieux-Marché Quarter.* The Deep South ambience is enhanced by the Spanish moss hanging from live oaks. The main local source of reve-

nue is the packing and shipping of oysters and shrimp, which grow to jumbo size in the Gulf. Shrimp boats dock at *Small Crafts Harbor* beyond the Hwy. in the old quarter.

SIGHTS

Beauvoir
Ten km west of Biloxi you can visit the house in which Jefferson Davis, the president of the Confederacy, spent the last 12 years of his life. Built in 1853, this is a handsome house, a shrine kept up by the idiosyncratic 'Sons of Confederate Veterans'. *Daily 9 am–4 pm; admission US $6; US Hwy. 90; Tel. 601/388-13 13*

RESTAURANT

Mary Mahoney's Old French House
❖ Enjoyed in the setting of this lovely house, which was built in 1737, regional Creole fish and shellfish specialities are simply too good to be true. *Mon–Sat dinner, 138 Rue Magnolia, Tel. 601/374-01 63, category 2*

HOTEL

Royal D'Iberville
A resort hotel on the beach with a variety of sport facilities and a restaurant. *264 rooms, 3420 W Beach Bd., Tel. 601/388-66 10, Fax 385-60 67, categories 1–2*

SURROUNDING AREA

West Ship Island (101/E5)
★ Part of a single island until Hurricane Camille split it into two in 1969, West Ship Island is just a huge sandbank and a fabulous place to swim and sun. In the background looms D-shaped *Fort Massachusetts,* a Civil War relic. Watch out for alligators in the island ponds. Otherwise there's nothing but sun, sand and sea. *Ferries leave Biloxi daily at 9 am and noon, leaving the island at 3.45 pm and, in summer, at 6.45 pm. The crossing takes 70 minutes each way, ticket US $12*

BIRMINGHAM

(101/F3) Alabama's biggest city exemplifies the transformation of the South. Once dubbed the Pittsburg of the South because it was a railway and steel centre and even despised as America's Johannesburg because segregation was so strictly enforced, Birmingham saw the launching of Project C (for *confrontation)* in 1963. Thousands of Civil Rights activists, including the Reverend Martin Luther King, were arrested. The headquarters of the protest movement was the *16th St. Baptist Church (between Sixth and Seventh Avs.),* which suffered a bombing assault by the Ku Klux Klan, when four people were killed. In 1974 the city elected its first African-American mayor. Today Birmingham is a booming metropolis, with much of its wealth coming from pharmaceuticals. The city's Iron Age is commemorated by the *Sloss Furnas Museum,* an old steel mill with blast furnaces, smelters and casting-pits. The men who once worked here used to say: If mules had to do this work, it would be illegal. *First Av./32nd St.; Tues–Sat 10 am–4 pm, Sun noon–4 pm; admission free*

HUNTSVILLE

(101/F2) Rarely do you see such a jumble of the Old and New South as Huntsville in northern Alabama. Two old residential sections of the city, the *Old Town* at *Courthouse Square* and the *Twickenham Historic District,* comprise the biggest cluster by far of *antebellum*-houses in the state of Alabama. One of these houses, *Weeden House,* dates from 1819 and is open to the public *(300 Gates Av., Tues–Sun 10 am–4 pm; admission US $4).* In addition, Huntsville is the place where the American Defence Department concentrated rocket research after World War II. In the aftermath of the war, it was a windfall for the US government to acquire the skills of the German rocket specialist Wernher von Braun and 118 colleagues who had collaborated during the war on the V-2 project in Peenemünde. After a short denazification period, or – in cold war parlance – debriefing, the German scientists were instrumental in developing the Redstone I rockets, which launched the first American satellites into space, and the Saturn V, which catapulted the first astronauts to the moon. An imposing high-rise complex called *New Huntsville* and next to it the *Von Braun Civic Center,* named after the pioneering German rocket scientist, attest to the prosperity which has been engendered by the *Marshall Space Flight Center.*

SIGHTS

Alabama Space and Rocket Center
★ The rockets stand tall here – a Saturn V is in a prone position to show its full, 40-m length – which made America the world leader in space. This is more interesting than the Kennedy Space Center in Florida because there is a replica of a Space Shuttle. A microgravity simulator will leave your stomach feeling as it does after a visit to the Disney World Tower of Terror. Breathtaking photos and exhibits highlight the astronauts' historic missions. *Daily 9 am–5 pm, in summer 8am– 6 pm; admission US $14; Hwy. 20 (via I 65), 8 km west of downtown*

HOTELS

In and near Huntsville numerous motels are operated by national chains, most in category 3.

Huntsville Hilton
A modern high-rise with a bar, restaurant, pool and jogging track. *284 rooms, 401 Williams Av., Tel. 205/533-14 40, Fax 533-60 02, category 2*

Sheraton Inn
Sheraton Inns are more modest and cheaper than normal Sheraton Hotels yet this one also has a pool, tennis, fitness center and golf. *146 rooms, 1000 Glenn Hearn Bd., Tel. 205/772-96 62, Fax 464- 91 16, category 2*

INFORMATION

Tourist Information Center
Daily 9 am–5 pm, in the Von Braun Civic Center, 700 Monroe St., Tel. 205/ 533-01 25, Fax 536-90 04

SURROUNDING AREA

TVA   (101/F2)
Like a barrette across a ponytail, dams above, to the east and to the west restrain the Tennessee River. In 1935 the TVA, which stands for *Tennessee Valley Authority,* was set up by Act of Congress to generate electricity and create thousands of jobs in an attempt to combat the Depression.

MONTGOMERY

(101/F4) Alabama's capital and the only city in the southern part of the state with a population of more than a quarter of a million also boasts a Neo-Classical capitol building. Above it the Stars and Stripes still vie for pride of place with the Confederate flag. A bronze star marks the spot on which Jefferson Davis, the president of the Confederacy, took his oath of office. He was the man who is recorded as having said to a visitor: We recognize the negro exactly God and God's Book and God's Laws, in nature, tell us to recognize him – our inferior, fitted expressly for servitude. More on the first Confederate capital in the *First White House of the Confederacy,* 644 *Washington Av., Mon–Fri 8 am– 4.30 pm, Sat and Sun 9 am– 4.30 pm; admission free.*

NATCHEZ

(100/C4) ★ The French explorer La Salle claimed this site on the Mississippi in 1682 for France. The Natchez Indian tribe contested his country's claim to it and fought off the French in a fierce battle in 1729. The French defeated the Indians in 1731, selling any Natchez who didn't succeed in escaping them to the West Indies as slaves. The Treaty of Paris in 1763 ended the French and Indian War (the Anglo-French overseas theatre of operations in the European Seven Years' War), in which the Indians sided with the French against the English. French sources show that the Natchez called their chieftans Great Suns. As part of the Middle Mississippi culture, which is documented by remains in Louisiana dating from as early as 4,000 BC, the Natchez Indians were mound builders between 1,000 and 1,540 AD, when Hernando de Soto entered the Mississippi Valley and destroyed the sophisticated culture of this tribe just as the Conquistadors did in Mexico and South America. Remains of the prehistoric Natchez mounds and temples, which somewhat resemble Aztec ruins, can be viewed at *The Grand Village of Natchez (400 Jefferson Davis Bd., Mon–Sat 9 am–5 pm, Sun 1.30–5 pm; admission free).* During the antebellum 19th century Natchez was the boomtown capital of the Mississippi territory. Traders brought their wares along the dangerous *Natchez Trace,* to Natchez from Nashville, Tennessee. Rafts went downriver on the Mississippi to the sea from Natchez, which owed its prosperity to cotton and slave labour. By the time paddle-wheel steamers were plying the Mississippi, the plantation owners were immensely rich and Natchez was the world's biggest cotton port. At one time half of all American millionaires are said to have lived at Natchez, amassing art collections and big libraries. What made Natchez bow to Charleston, South Carolina, was the presence of the raw *Frontier,* the unexplored wilderness across the Mississippi. Below the prosperous city *Natchez-under-the-Hill,* sprang up near the river port with brothels and saloons where the only thing that was cheaper here than a woman's body was a man's life. All that's left of Sodom on the Mississippi is a small quarter with bars and restaurants. The rest has been destroyed by mudslides and flooding. After the Civil War Natchez fell into a charmed sleep that has left it almost as it was in antebellum days.

SIGHTS

The Natchez Pilgrimage

In the 1930s two ladies' clubs, The Pilgrimage Garden Club and the Natchez Garden Club, squabbled fiercely over the right to cultivate local tradition. After hostilities finally ceased, the two groups joined forces to form The Natchez Pilgrimage. Since then, three times a year, in *March/April,* in *October* and at *Christmas,* six groups of five historic houses each are opened to the public in the morning and afternoon. In addition, two houses are shown by candlelight on alternate evenings under the auspices of the *Confederate Pageant* with music and dancing. The ladies of the

Pilgrimage carry huge parasols and wear hoop skirts and crinolines of the type familiar from the 1939 film of 'Gone with the Wind'. During the rest of the year, six historic Natchez houses are open to the public *daily from 9 am–5 pm.* Only the 17 ground-floor rooms were ever finished at *Longwood (140 Lower Woodville Rd.),* which was laid out on an octagonal plan. Dr. Haller Nutt, a supporter of the Union, is said to have died of a broken heart after the Union soldiers he had taken care of burned down his plantation and cotton gin. At the corner of Pearl St./Monroe St. is *Stanton Hall,* with a huge ballroom and English antiques, the headquarters of the Pilgrimage and the finest of all the antebellum mansions in Natchez. Four rooms in it accommodate paying guests. *The Burn (712 N Union St.)* is in the Neo-Classical style, called Greek Revival here. It boasts lovely gardens and also has rooms for guests. *Melrose* on Melrose Av., is a gem of early 19th-century Southern architecture and has lovely gardens. The *Natchez Trace* starts on Allicott Hill, at *Connelly's Tavern,* built in 1798, where no more than five persons might sleep in one bed. *The Briars,* furnished in Oriental, English and European antiques, is further from the historic district. In 1845, after a chequered career as an officer (West Point, class of 1828) and a planter, Jefferson Davis celebrated his second marriage here – to Varina Howell, a *Southern belle. Pilgrimage Headquarters, Stanton Hall Grounds, 410 N Commerce St., P.O. Box 347, Natchez, MS 39120, Tel. 601/446-66 31 and 800/647-67 42*

Carriage House

In the Stanton Hall grounds *Southern fried chicken* and *ham,* real old Southern cooking. Bread baked on the premises. *Lunch and dinner daily, closed on holidays, 401 High St., Tel. 601/445-51 51, category 3*

Cock of the Walk

〰 A superb view of the Mississippi and spicy Cajun and Creole specialities like catfish, crayfish, shrimp and gumbo *(always with okra). Mon–Sat dinner, 15 Silver St., Tel. 601/446-89 20, category 3*

Several of the antebellum Southern mansions are also Bed & Breakfasts. Book well in advance through Natchez Pilgrimage.

The Briars

★ The Howell house. Here the 18-year-old Varina, the 'Mississippi Rose', celebrated her marriage in 1845 to the man who would become the president of the Confederate States 16 years later: Jefferson Davis. Granted historic monument status, this fine house in the (1818) Federal style, with its columned porch, beautiful 〰 views of the Mississippi and individually decorated rooms, is one of the most romantic places to stay in the South. Smoking is prohibited in the rooms and frowned on even in the hall and on the porch. *13 rooms, 31 Irving Lane, Tel. 601/446-96 54, Fax 445-60 37, category 1*

Natchez Eola

Built in 1927, the Natchez Eola fell into genteel decline but was restored in the 1960s, reopening in 1980.

From the rooms there are ⬇ views of the Mississippi or the lovely inner courtyard. Bar and two restaurants. This is the only hotel in Mississippi to be short-listed as a Historic Hotel of America. *125 rooms, 110 N Pearl St., Tel. 601/445-6000, Fax 446-53 10, categories 1–3*

SURROUNDING AREA

Natchez Trace Parkway (100–101 / C-F4–1)

On the outskirts of the city begins a two-lane road to *Nashville,* Tennessee. Settlers, mail riders, traders and fugitive convicts used to walk or ride the 720 km of the original track, which went through unsettled Indian country. A French word has survived here instead of the English 'track' (trace derives from French *tracer,* to track down or mark out a path; noun: la trace). Nature reserves on both sides of the road afford ⬇ superb views where the forests are not too dense. Wild animals are protected, panels tell the history of the area and trails are posted. The drive from Natchez to *Tupelo* in northeastern Mississippi takes about 7 hours if you don't linger along the way.

Tracks through the swamp: Natchez Trace

71

New Orleans is unique

French charm, lacy wrought-iron balconies, jazz, blues,
Mardi Gras and Creole cuisine

Here you're down South but it's an entirely different kettle of fish. New Orleans is called the *Big Easy,* which aptly describes the heady atmosphere of the city Europeans view as 'America's European Masterpiece'. It's no more – and no less – European than several other US cities. A unique blend of French, Caribbean and Spanish culture, New Orleans is, incidentally, one of the world's largest ports. US businessmen prefer this city to any other for conventions and it's easy to see why: leisurely business lunches featuring Creole cuisine and so much to do in the evenings. With *antebellum*-charm backed by a booming *Sunbelt economy,* New Orleans is lifestyle writ large. The bayou region is known as *Cajun Country,* home to a culture that is fittingly characterized by the expression *joie de vivre.* The descendants of French settlers in what are now the Canadian provinces of Nova Scotia and New Brunswick, Ca-

juns speak a form of 17th-century French. They fled *l'Acadie,* even before their Canadian home was ceded to Britain in 1763. The word Cajun is the slurred pronounciation used by their English-speaking neighbours for *acadien.*

Northern Louisiana is the only part of the state which is really Deep South. Even Louisiana residents differentiate between the two cultures and regions in their state. With sugar-cane already a lucrative crop in the southeastern Delta, the Louisiana territory was purchased for US $15,000,000 from France by Thomas Jefferson's administration in 1803.

Arkansas, pronounced arkinsaw, which some English speakers may not have known before the Clinton administration, is another state which is only historically part of the South. Geographically speaking, it should be assigned to the Great Plains, the vast prairie that stretches west of the Mississippi on up to Canada. However, Arkansas opted to join the Confederacy. In 1957 its capital, Little Rock, was the scene of the first serious armed clash between a segregationist South-

Lacy balconies, jazz and
Cajun — a café in
New Orleans' Bourbon Street

ern state government and the Federal government trying to implement Civil Rights legislation. After Arkansas Governor Orval Faubus, an upholder of the doctrine of 'states' rights', had called out National Guard troops to prevent black children from attending the four Little Rock high schools, President Dwight D. Eisenhower dispatched a thousand paratroopers of the 101st Airborne Division to Little Rock.

BATON ROUGE

(100/C5) To readers of the Pulitzer Prize winning novel *All the King's Men,* based in part on the career of Huey Long, governor of Louisiana, the Capitol is a reminder of this populist politician, who is buried in front of it. Assassinated in 1935, Huey Long was a demagogue, a grass-roots socialist for some and for others a home-grown Fascist. His autobiography took its title, 'Every Man a King', from a speech made by William Jennings Bryan, the fundamentalist Tennessee state prosecutor at the Scopes trial. In *Life on the Mississippi,* Mark Twain had mocked the Baton Rouge

Capitol as a sham castle inspired by Sir Walter Scott's historical romances. Since Huey Long decreed that no building in the state might be higher than his new Capitol, the ☀ view from the 27th-floor observation deck is unobstructed. *Daily 8 am–4 pm; admission free*

LITTLE ROCK

(100/C2) The capital of Arkansas has been noticed recently by the international media for the first time since 1957, this time as Bill Clinton's birthplace. Race riots are a thing of the past. This quiet small city (pop. 175,000) is not particularly remarkable to look at except for its pretty *Riverfront Park* on *Arkansas River* and majestic *Old State House.* The most interesting things to see in Arkansas are outside the capital. Attractions of the Wonder State include a romantic old spa *with hot springs* in *Hot Springs National Park* at the foot of the *Oachita Mountains* and the *Ozark Mountains* north of Little Rock, the most scenic mountains east of the Rockies. Crystal clear lakes and rivers invite you to explore them by canoe and on foot. Ozark folklore (Country

Music) is lovingly presented in the *Ozark Folk Center* in the town of *Mountain View*.

**Arkansas Department
of Parks and Tourism**
Mon–Fri 9 am–5 pm, 1 Capitol Mall, Little Rock, AR 72201, Tel. 501/ 682-10 88, Fax 682-13 64

NATCHITOCHES

(100/B4) ★ This is the site of the earliest settlement in Louisiana, pronounced Natchetish, on the Red River. If the film 'Steel Magnolias' had not been made here in 1988, it would have remained unkown outside the US. However, as 'Chinquapin', it became world famous. Its hidden secret is a lovely old and virtually pristine *French Quarter* along *Front St.,* where the houses sport lavish wrought-iron balconies, paved inner courtyards and spiral stairs. Four years older than New Orleans, this is a quiet microcosm of that flamboyant city.

Lasyone's Meat Pie Kitchen
Natchitoches is famous for meat pies. You'll find the best ones in this unpretentious restaurant. *Daily 11 am–9 pm, 622 2nd St., Tel. 318/352-33 53, category 3*

Clouthier Townhouse
Bed & Breakfast in the historic quarter with ❧ views of old *Front St.* and *Cane River Lake. 2 rooms, 8 Ducournau St., Tel. and Fax 318/352-54 42, category 2*

NEW ORLEANS
☛ **City Map inside back cover**

(101/D6) At the door of the Old Absinthe House a sign flatters the ladies and lures the gentlemen: The world's most beautiful women pass through this door. A fitting introduction to this beguiling city.

The cradle of jazz pulses all night and all day with Dixieland, jazz, rock, Cajun, zydeco and blues and not just in Bourbon Street. *French Quarter* Dixieland bands recreate this early, 1900s style of jazz, made famous by the Original Dixieland Jazz Band, formed about 1911 by five New Orleans musicians. Taken over by white jazz musicians in Chicago during the 1920s, Dixieland has retained the original instrumentation: trumpet, clarinet, trombone, drums and piano. Blues was made popular during the 1920s and 30s by black women singers. From the Mississippi Delta came a different kind of blues, the creation of black men like the immortal Leadbelly, Blind Lemon Jefferson and Son House, the father of Delta blues. Almost as distinctive as the personal and local styles of jazz, blues and dance music are the subtle variations in Creole haute cuisine and Cajun cooking, the latter loosely defined as fiery hot vegetable sauces for shrimp and chicken, all of them rich, served with rice and beans, the soul food of slaves blended with the food preferred by the early Spanish colonists and later French settlers.

Since the original European settlers here were Roman Catholics, the custom of celebrating Carnival before the austerity of

Lent has been retained in the syncopated form of Mardi Gras, enriched, like the city's cuisine, with overtones of African mysticism and Latin-American rhythms. In the mid-19th century the city authorities made ineffectual attempts to suppress Carnival. However, a group of influential townspeople founded the Mystick Krewe of Comus, Merrie Monarch of Mirth, to organize revels with a parade and masquerade ball. Other Krewes, notably the Rex, were formed and Carnival took on contours that would be recognizable today. After the Civil War it flouted Reconstruction. Carnival season begins on *Epiphany, 6 January,* culminating in the two weeks before Fat Tuesday (Shrove Tuesday). On Shrove Tuesday the krewes parade down *St. Charles Av.* and *Canal St.* The Mardi Gras parade is organized by the Rex Krewe, who elect the Monarch. *Walking Clubs* of teenagers precede the Rex. Elsewhere the Black Krewe of Zulu with the *Big Shot of Africa* hands out coconuts instead of doubloons. In the evening the Comus Krewe marches by torchlight. By Ash Wednesday everything is over. *(Hotels must be booked months in advance!)*

Hurray! Finally a city not laid out on that 18th-century grid so reminiscent of Roman army camps! *Canal St.* roughly bisects the city. Everything upriver from it is known as *uptown* and everything downriver is *downtown.* Street names change erratically at Canal St., a disconcerting reminder of the days when the city with its residential areas was distinctly divided into English-speaking and French-speaking sections.

The oldest buildings are in the *Vieux Carré,* the *French Quarter,* with its little stuccoed houses and French roofs. When the Spanish took over the region, quite a few of these were replaced by patrician townhouses with inner courtyards. By the early 19th century the two styles had merged. The celebrated wrought-iron balconies are a feature common to both traditions. Later they were picked up and lavishly used by the builders of the grand mansions in the English-speaking residential section called the *Garden District.*

New Orleans was founded by the French in 1718 as part of their vast colonial territory extending up the entire length of the Mississippi Valley. Many of the first French settlers were, as was so often the case in 18th-century French and English colonies, convicts, debtors, smugglers and camp followers. From 1763 the Delta was ceded to Spain by Britain under the terms of the Treaty of Paris after the French and Indian war. The word *creole* is used narrowly in the US to refer to New Orleans descendants of the early French settlers. The French word is thought to derive from the Spanish criollo – domestically born and bred, and includes those born in the West Indies of African, Spanish and French descent. In 1768 the first anti-colonial revolt in what was to become the US was quelled by Spanish forces under Alexander O'Reilly. In 1803 the colony was ceded to France. Napoleon sold it to the US three weeks later. *Kaintucks* – the Yankees, who in the eyes of the creoles all came from Kentucky, governed hence forth. Today New Orleans is a thriving port city, with oil refineries, banking and tourism contributing to its prosperity. Latter-day *Kaintucks* have not been allowed to put a thoroughfare through the *Vieux Carré.*

SIGHTS

Aquarium of the Americas (U/D5)

A memorable experience for adults and children alike and an absolute must for families! *Daily 9.30 am–6 pm; admission adults US $10,50, children US $5; at the end of Canal St. on the Mississippi; Tel. 504/581-46 29*

French Quarter/Vieux Carré

★ The heart of New Orleans is a marvellous place for wandering about in and exploring because it is smaller and more compressed than it appears at first. The presence of delicate wrought-iron balconies, stuccoed facades, high walls and enclosed courtyards will guide you. Where they stop the quarter ends. For those who don't mind poring over maps it's bounded by *Canal St., Esplanade Av., Louis Armstrong Park* and *Mississippi.*

Right at the centre of things is *Jackson Square* (**U/D-E3**) with its late 18th-century Spanish architecture. The earliest French houses were destroyed by fires that swept the city in 1788 and 1794. The square planted with gardens and bounded on three sides by broad pavements might be a good place to start exploring the surrounding area. But before you do, enjoy a soup-bowl-sized cup of chicory-flavoured café au lait and whisper-light beignets – nun's sighs – to go with it. Carnival reigns all year round here. Buskers, sidewalk artists, acrobats and purveyors of kitsch keep things lively. Northwest of Jackson Square is *St. Louis Cathedral* (**U/D2–3**), the third Roman Catholic church to have been built on the site. A blend of Neo-Romanesque and Neo-Baroque, it boasts three towers and a *Cathedral Garden.* The building next to it which sports such a magnificent balcony is the *Cabildo* (**U/D3**), once the seat of the Spanish colonial government. St. Peter and St. Ann Streets are notable for the three-storey *Pontalba Buildings,* (**U/D-E3-2**) houses and commercial buildings dating from 1850. *No. 523* in *St. Ann St.,* a superb New Orleans French house, is open to the public. *(Tues–Sun 10 am–5 pm; admission US $4).*

From *Moon Walk,* (**U/E3**) a boardwalk beyond Decatur St., you can see ↘ the harbour basins and ocean-going tankers. A few paces back in the other direction, downriver from Jackson Square in *Decatur St.,* is the old *French Market* (**U/E–F2**) dating from 1720. The real fruit and vegetable market is in *N Peters*

Street sounds buskers in New Orleans

St. (**U/F2**), where the *flea market* is set out at weekends. The restored *French Market* is now a complex housing restaurants, shops and boutiques, some selling junk and souvenirs and others very stylish.

Bounding the French Quarter is oak-lined *Esplanade Av.* (**U/E-F 1-2**) with its large mansions. Where it begins, at the *Old US Mint* (**U/F2**), there is a *Jazz Museum,* which doesn't stop at music history. It has an exhibition on Mardi Gras and even one on the tram called Desire dating from 1906 (which gave its name to Tennessee Williams' play 'A Streetcar Named Desire'). (**U/F2**, *Wed–Sun 10 am–5 pm; admission US $3*).

Of the thoroughfares running through the French Quarter from Esplanade Av. to Canal St., *Chartres St.* (**U/C-F4-1**) has suffered the most from demolition and the inroads of mass tourism. Two old houses on it are *Napoleon House* (**U/D3**) *No. 500,* now a bar, and *No. 514* is the reconstruction of an *apothecary's,* the *Historical Pharmaceutical Museum.* (**U/D3**, *Tues–Sun 10 am–5 pm; admission US $3*). A block away, at *No. 440,* is *Maspero's*

Exchange (**U/D3**), also a bar but it's in a house dating from 1788, built just after the great fire.

Old *Royal St.* (**U/C-F4-1**), however, has (all but one block) remained just as it was, lined with mansions and handsome commercial buildings. *No. 417,* an early 19th-century mansion, now houses the famous *Brennan's Restaurant* (**U/C3**). Queues of hopefuls form in front of it in the mornings. Another is *Nr. 534,* the fine *Merieult House,* which goes back to 1792, in which the *Historic New Orleans Collection* (**U/D3**) is exhibited, an elegant slant on the civic museum. *(Tues–Sun 10 am–5 pm; admission free).* Across from it is *Maison Seignouret,* which dates from 1816.

Two other famous streets, *Royal St.* and *Bourbon St.* (**U/C-E4-1**) are closed to car traffic most of the day. This is where all the best known bars, jazz clubs and nightclubs are (most opened during the day as well). At the *corner of St. Louis St.* (**U/D3**) things are really humming. Not only are there two Napoleon Houses in New Orleans. *Bourbon St.* is blessed with two *Old Absinthe Houses;* absinthe, being poisonous,

Mark Twain would have felt right at home: the sternwheeler 'Natchez'

is no longer served. The one at *No. 240* (**U/C3**) is the original Absinthe House, which goes back to 1806, whereas the other, at *No. 400*, took over the name with the bar furnishings from No. 240 during Prohibition. Near the bars there are two more fine old houses, the *Hermann-Grima House* (1831), very much in the style of Old Savannah, Georgia at *No. 820, St. Louis St.*, and *Casa Hove* (1740), which now houses an elegant shop selling perfumes, at No. 723, Toulouse St. (**U/D2–3**)

RIVERBOAT EXCURSIONS

The Steamboat Natchez, (almost) an authentic sternwheel steamer, plies up and down the Mississippi. Another takes you through the bayous as far as *Baratoria*, the Cajun pirate's hideway, and is, of course, named after him: Bayou Jean Lafitte. (Both dock at *Toulouse Street Wharf below Jackson Square* (**U/E3**); the *Natchez: daily 11.30 am and 2.30 pm, US $ 14,75; Bayou Jean Lafitte: daily 11 am, US $35*). For a free ride take the *Canal Street Ferry* from Canal St. to Algiers Point on the far bank of the Mississippi: an interesting, approx 20-minute trip on the appropriately named *Old Man River.*

RESTAURANTS

Acme Oyster House
Oysters on the half shell at a marble-topped counter. Popular with policemen and they're in the know. *Daily 11 am–10.30 pm, 724 Iberville St., Tel. 504/522-59 73, category 3*

Antoine's
★ New Orleans' world-famous restaurant founded back in

1840. French and Creole cuisine in the grand Old World dining room. *Mon–Sat lunch and dinner, 713 St. Louis St., Tel. 504/581-44 22, category 2*

Café du Monde
Beignets and café au lait. The most popular place of its kind, especially for French-style breakfasts. *Daily 1 am–midnight, 813 Decatur St., Tel. 504/525-45 44, category 3*

Commander's Palace
In a Victorian mansion in the Gordon District, with tables outside. Highly imaginative French and American cuisine and on Sundays a jazz brunch. *Daily 11 am–11 pm, closed for Mardi Gras and on holidays, 1403 Washington Av., Tel. 504/899-82 21, category 1*

Dooky Chase
Extraordinary Creole cooking but in a dangerous part of town. Take a taxi there and back! *Daily lunch and dinner, 2301 Orleans St., Tel. 504/821-22 94, category 2*

The Jackson Brewery
A varied menu in the Food Court in a restored fin de siècle brewery *Daily 9 am–11 pm, Decatur St. at Jackson Square, Tel. 504/529-12 11, categories 2–3*

K-Paul's Louisiana Kitchen
You can't make reservations here so you'll have to queue up with everybody else. Is the long wait worth it? The real thing, the most authentic Cajun cuisine, featuring seafood, in *French Quarter* for your delectation. *Mon–Sat 11.30 am–2.30 pm and 5 pm–11 pm, 416 Chartres St., Tel. 504/524-73 94, category 1*

The categories do not hold for the two weeks of *Mardi Gras*, the *Jazz Festival* and the big football events. At those times a 3–5 day stay will set costs considerably more than at other times. *Info: Tel. 800/672-61 24, www.neworleanscvb.com*

Bourbon New Orleans
Historic hotel with a pool, a ballroom, a music bar, restaurant and superb service. *211 rooms, 717 Orleans St., Tel. 504/523-22 22, Fax 572-46 66, category 1*

Holiday Inn French Quarter
Ideally located yet still affordable. An indoor pool, a restaurant and parking facilities. *332 rooms, 124 Royal St., Tel. 504/529-72 11, Fax 566-11 27, category 2*

Maison Dupuy
A somewhat austerely restored early luxury hotel in seven old French Quarter houses with restaurants, a bar, a heated pool, a fitness centre and parking facilities. *194 rooms, 1001 Toulouse St., Tel. 504/586-80 00, Fax 525-53 34, categories 1–2*

Monteleone
Built in 1886, the hotel was completely renovated in 1996 but has remained the grand hotel of the French Quarter. Spacious, handsomely furnished rooms, some of them with *brass beds,* and others with *fourposter beds (tester beds).* A Neo-Baroque facade and a revolving bar in the lobby. *635 rooms, 214 Royal St., Tel. 504/523-33 41, Fax 528-10 19, category 1*

Prytania Park
An unpretentious-looking hotel in the Garden District but what makes it so special are the 13 rooms in the restored Victorian townhouse which is part of the hotel complex. *62 rooms, 1525 Pry-tania St., Tel. 504/524-04 27, Fax 522-29 77, category 3*

Le Richelieu
An enchanting house in the French Quarter. Some rooms have balconies and others big, naughty mirrors. An intimate bar, café, pool and free parking. *86 rooms, 1234 Chartres St., Tel. 504/529-24 92, Fax 524-81 79, category 2*

Absinthe Bar
A dark little bar with the original furnishings of the real Old Absinthe House. Great jazz as well as rhythm & blue. Worth a visit just to see the bar. *Every evening, Fri and Sat usually a low admission charge, 400 Bourbon St., Tel. 504/525-81 08*

Café Brasil
Popular bands draw big crowds but modern jazz is just for hardcore fans. A great place for dancing, also at Mardi Gras. *Opening times vary daily, 2100 Chartres St., Tel. 504/947-93 86*

The Dream Palace
A resurrected hippie joint, this club is worked by all sorts of bands and combos, mostly modern. *Wed–Sun from 10.30 pm, 534 Frenchmen St., Tel. 504/944-41 80*

Howlin' Wolf
Alternative rock, modern country music, open microphone on Mondays in what was once a cotton warehouse. Jam sessions. *Daily 3 pm–3 am, 828 S Peters St., Tel. 504/523-25 51*

A different New Orleans: Aquarium of the Americas

Palm Court Jazz Café

Ring up and find out what's on: frequent programme changes. A venue – occasionally – for hearing the best jazz and rhythm & blues groups. *Wed–Sun 7 pm–11 pm, 1204 Decatur St., Tel. 504/525-02 00*

Preservation Hall

'Dusty and old', as the jazzmen say about the famous pieces they perform. Packed. *Daily from 8 pm, admission US $4 and US $1–$5 for request numbers, 726 St. Peter St., Tel. 504/522-28 41*

Tipitina's

✻ Reggae, rock, rhythm & blues and Cajun live. The city's favourite music venue. *Daily from about 8 pm, 501 Napoleon Av., Tel. 504/897-39 43*

INFORMATION

Visitor Information Service

Headquarters of the *State Office of Tourism* and the *Greater New Orleans Tourist and Convention Commission. Daily 9 am–5 pm, 334 Royal St., Tel. 504/566-50 11, Fax 522-61 23*

SURROUNDING AREA

Cajun Country   (100–101 / B–D6)

★ The Delta is Cajun Country: much of it swamps, the home of French settlers who migrated from New Brunswick and Nova Scotia in the 18th century. Many Acadians drowned at sea or on the overland trek to the Delta. Until the 1950s oil boom the Cajuns were cut off from their neighbours, living from hunting and fishing. During the 1980s oil bust, the bayou country went into a recession. Widening and straightening of the bayous has accelerated land erosion and the silting up of the waterways, endangering Cajun livelihoods and the wetlands ecosystem. In places like *Lafayette* and *Houma* Cajun culture has survived on the motto: *Lâche pas la potate* (Don't let go of the potato).

Hill country, bluegrass, bourbon

Graceland, the shrine – the King of the castle

Hill country, the *Mountain South,* comprises the Southern States of Kentucky and Tennessee – but mountains aren't the whole story here. Kentucky's most attractive region is the rugged eastern part of the state dotted with little old towns in the Bluegrass Downs, where bourbon whiskey is distilled and throughbreds graze in lush fields. The state is bounded in the west by the Mississippi and the broad plains sloping down to it. Tennessee certainly has three distinct regions. Like Kentucky mountainous in the east, Tennessee boasts Great Smoky Mountains National Park, shared with North Carolina. The middle part of this surprisingly narrow state, which only measures 160 km from north to south, used to be plantation country in the best Southern tradition.

Western Tennessee is, like Kentucky, part of the Mississippi Valley. Tennessee's biggest city, Memphis, has always been a major river port. Their geographical situation caused both Kentucky and Tennessee political headaches in the past. Against the will of traders and sharecroppers in eastern Tennessee, the planters muscled the state into the Confederacy. Kentucky never joined it and Tennessee was the last state to secede from the Union. The battle of Nashville (15–16 December 1864), at which black soldiers, too, distinguished themselves in the Union cause, saw Confederate troops routed by a Unionist Virginian general.

Tennessee recovered fairly well from the after-effects of the Civil War. Agriculture was mechanized here earlier in the 20th century than in many parts of the South. However, soil erosion and flooding by the Tennessee River led farmers to migrate to the towns. The New Deal in the 1930s, which the Roosevelt administration launched to revitalize the US economy, had the effect of accelerating the flight from the land. Only very recently have there been any signs at all of the trend being reversed. Modern industrial complexes like the General Motors Saturn plant south of Nashville have been built on green-field sites in once predominantly rural areas. However, be-

Indian summer:
autumn ablaze in Tennessee

tween the rolling hills that are part of the western Appalachian System and the beginning of the Great Plains, Kentucky's cities have not yet begun to sprawl into the conurbations that mar so much of the Atlantic seaboard.

CHATTANOOGA

(102/C4) Chattanooga Choo-Choo is an old Glenn Miller favourite. Seldom has a place been so identified with a song as Chattanooga in southern Tennessee. Passenger trains no longer stop here. No more *Choo-Choo me home.* Yet the city cultivates both railroad tradition and the history of swing. The *Choo-Choo Complex,* in the old (1909) Southern Railroad station, is now a *Holiday Inn Hotel (327 rooms, 1400 N Market St., Tel. 423/266-5000, Fax 265-4635, category 2).* The old waiting room is the hotel lobby and some cars have even been turned into hotel suites. The original Choo-Choo steam engine is surrounded by souvenir shops and cafés. And you can take a nostalgic ride on a steam-engine driven train out from this city, which is so gracefully tucked into a bend of the

Tennessee River. What is left of the old *Tennessee Valley Railroad* runs for about 10 km *(stations 220 Chamberlain Av. and 4119 Cromwell Rd., Tel. 423/894-8028).* They have been restored in 1930s style. Choochoo! But of course, country music reigns supreme here now and long may it reign.

GREAT SMOKY MOUNTAINS NATIONAL PARK

☛ Map on page 108/109

(103/D–E3–4) ★ This nature reserve, which covers more than 2000 square km, does live up to its name. The highest peaks rise to 1,500–2,200 m. They are part of North America's geologically oldest mountain system, formed more than 230 million years ago. At least a third of the Park is virgin forest and rain forest to boot. It steams in the sun when plants transpire and secrete volatile oils, giving off clouds of bluish smoke. Black bears wander through these woods but you're not likely to catch sight of one because they're too cagey to tangle with people. They do occasionally help themselves to campers' provisions. You don't need to be addicted to Gary Larson's cartoons to know that, if you're camping out, hang your food supplies up between two trees as high as you can and not too close to your camp site. The Park is accessible from Tennessee via *Gatlinburg* on US Hwy. 441 and from North Carolina via *Cherokee,* also on US Hwy. 441. From US Hwy. 441 the Little River Rd. branches off to the southwest and *Cades Cove.* At least 1,500 km of posted trails start at parking lots (car parks). The *Appalachian Trail* runs through the Park. If you want to camp out, you'll have to go to one of the *Visitors Centers* at the entrances to the Park and obtain – free of charge – a *backcountry permit.* US visitors to the Park – more than 9 million a year – come here from late March to mid-May and again in the latter half of October. At those times roads, picnic spots and camping sites are packed, particularly at weekends. Spring, when the rhododendron is in bloom, and autumn, when the foliage is changing, are lovely times to be here though the weather can be warm. A popular place to hike to is ✲ *Clingmans Dome,* at 2,025 m the highest peak in the Park. It is often veiled in a bluish haze (the road goes almost to the top). Another is *Mount Le Conte* and, taking you to it, the *Ahem Cave Trail,* which passes through *Laurels Hell,* a treeless but almost impenetrable jungle of mountain laurel and rhododendron.

Accommodation: in *Gatlinburg* – a cluster of hotels and souvenir shops – there are about 30,000 hotel beds in all three categories. The *Cherokee Indian Reservation* also has 70 camp sites and motels and isn't quite so overrun, even at peak season. An unpretentiously rustic but comfortable alternative is the *Buckhorn Inn (60 rooms, 3 cottages, Tel. 615/436-4668, no Fax, category 3).* For peace and quiet, the town of *Townsend,* Tennessee, with 90 basic camp sites off the beaten track but – not *Cades Cove, Elkmont* and *Smokemont!* – are recommended.

Bicycle hire: at *Cades Cove Campground, Tel. 423/436-5615.* Sat from sunrise to 10 am the road is reserved for cyclists. Information: *Sugarlands Visitor Center, beyond Gatlinburg; Oconaluftee Visitor Center, past Cherokee; Cades Cove Visitor Center, in Cades Cove.* For maps, hiking trails, car routes, bridle paths, information on flora and fauna or on anything else: *Tel. 423/436-1200, daily 8 am–5 pm (winter), 8 am–6 pm (spring, autumn), 8 am–7 pm (summer)*

LEXINGTON

(103/D2) Despite its size (pop. 200,000), this city has retained a rural atmosphere, not surprisingly so since its traditional sources of revenue are tobacco and horses. Downtown bristles with modern office buildings, hotels and shopping malls. Far more attractive is – to the northeast – the surrounding horse country. White domes above ★ *bluegrass meadows,* thoroughbreds and *antebellum* mansions are along the *Paris Pike* and the *Ironworks Pike.* Visitors are welcome at the old-fashioned *Keeneland Racecourse,* which is still without a loudspeaker system.

Here you can watch racehorses warming up from *April to October* every morning *(daily from sunrise to 9.30 am; admission free)* and, in the afternoons, racing *(daily 1 pm; admission US $2–$5),* really a treat. Because the market is so competitive and blood stock so valuable – stud fees of more than US $25,000 are no longer a rarity – horse breeders have had to banish visitors from stud-farms, which is a pity. The notable exception is the *Spendthrift Farm,* open to the public Feb–Jun *(884 Ironworks Pike, Tel. 606/225-20 03, Mon–Sat 10 am–2 pm; admission free).* Horse lovers shouldn't miss the *Kentucky Horse Park,* with a museum of equine history and more than 30 different breeds *(May-Oct daily, Nov–Apr Wed and Sun 9 am–5 pm; admission US $7.95; 4089 Ironworks Pike).*

RESTAURANT

High on Rose Cantina
❂ A real Tex-Mex (sounds like it, too) dinner. *301 E High St., Tel. 606/252-94 98, category 3*

HOTEL

Kimball House Motel
An unpretentious boarding-house. *10 rooms, 267 S Limestone St., Tel. 606/252-95 65, no Fax, category 3*

LOUISVILLE

(102/C2) An industrial city with a thriving service-sector (pharmaceuticals and the managed health-care industry) with skyscrapers jostling old warehouses and factories. The headquarters of the Humana hospital chain is located here, at *500 Main St.,* the sumptuous *Humana Building,* resplendent in marble and boasting authentic (!) Roman statues, attesting to the high (profit) margins to be made in this service-sector growth industry *(guided tours Sat 10 am–1.30 pm; admission free, and a ❧ panoramic view across the Ohio River from the 25th-floor observation platform).* But what brings most visitors to Louisville is racing. Since 1875 the *Kentucky Derby* has taken place annually on the first Saturday in May. Three-year-olds round the 1 ¼ miles (2 km) track for US $ 581,000 to the first to cross the finish line. Not just a sporting event, the Derby is the social event of the year. Hotel rooms are booked up then. Grandstand tickets are not to be had. For those thrilling two minutes of track time you can buy tickets on the day of the race for just US $20, standing room only, but you won't see all that much.

Accommodation: except for the Derby weeks Louisville has a wide selection of reasonably priced motels. For the brief Derby season the only thing to do is to book in advance from: *Kentucky Homes, 1431 St. James Court, Louisville, KY 40208, Tel. 502/635-72 41.*

Information on the Derby: *Churchill Downs, 700 Central Av., Louisville KY 40208, Tel. 502/636-44 00*

SURROUNDING AREA

Bardstown   (102/C2)
60 km south of Louisville is the town of *Bardstown,* where a Baptist preacher is said to have distilled the first bourbon whiskey from sour mash (corn) and spring water. At *Clermont,* 20 km

west of Bardstown, the *Jim Beam Distillery* is open to the public *(Mon–Sat 9 am–4.30 pm, Sun 1 pm–4 pm; admission free)*. Thirty km south of Bardstown, at *Loretto,* you can't miss the much smaller, lovingly restored *Maker's Mark Distillery (Mon–Sat 10.30 am–3.30 pm, Jan and Feb Sa closed; admission free)*. However, you won't be able to taste the elixir distilled by this old family business. The place is – like most of rural Kentucky – bone-dry.

Fort Knox (102/C2)

Nobody can go in there and you can't even linger more than five minutes in the street near it, even at a safe distance. This is the legendary treasure vault, the US government *Bullion Depository,* in which gold bars are kept in reserve, all 4 million kg of them, behind cyclone fences with gun turrets and doors weighing twenty tonnes. *On US Hwy. 31 W 50 km southwest of Louisville*

This isn't moonshine:
Maker's Mark Distillery

MEMPHIS

(102/A4) You think of Mississippi riverboats, rock & roll and Elvis and forget that Tennessee's biggest city is the 16th largest in the US. A prosperous one, with the world's largest Cotton Exchange, and still a major river port, shipping timber and soya beans (when a trade war isn't on with the European Union) to the planet, as the US is the largest producer of this controversial staple. But blues, country and rock & roll are still alive and kicking. So *put on your blue suede shoes.*

SIGHTS

Graceland

★ Way before your time? Didn't join the screamin' fans when He ruled the world? This is the shrine! Elvis' Southern dream castle. Elvis' suits: must be seen to be believed. His tomb: sob! His enterprising manager, one Phillips, sold the King to RCA for US $35,000. Phillips made millions on other rockabilly singers like Carl Perkins and the ever youthful Jerry Lee Lewis but Elvis was pure gold and tenderly loved. You'll never be the same after a pilgrimage to Graceland. *Daily 9 am–5 pm; admission US $7.95 (house only), US $14.95 (house, plane, museum and tour bus); 3734 Elvis Presley Bd.; Tel. 901/332-33 22 (bookings must be placed aeons in advance)*

RESTAURANT

Leonard's

Memphis proudly claims to be the *Pork Barbecue Capital of the*

Elvis' uniform, admired by the faithful

World, and this doesn't mean that Texas Chainsaw stuff, either. Of roughly 100 restaurants specializing in pork barbecue, this is the place to go, an institution. If gnawing on bones puts you off, sink your teeth into some delicious *outside brown* (grilled pork mince). *1140 Bellevue Bd. S, Tel. 901/948-15 81, opening hours vary, category 3*

HOTEL

The Peabody

★ In the midst of all those upstart Holiday Inns, Omnis and Marriotts, this is the grande dame (1925) of hotels, refurbished in the Neo-Renaissance style and again home to ducks, who waddle every morning from their penthouse suite to the marble fountain in the lobby. *452 rooms, 149 Union St., Tel. 901/529-40 00, Fax 529-41 84, category 1*

ENTERTAINMENT

Elvis' days live on in memory and those of Johnny Ace and Bobby Bland are but an evening gone. Tourists want to relive them and so they go to *Beale St.* and *Overton Square.*

BB King's Blues Club

⚑ Opened in 1991. Blues 7 nights a week; sometimes with BB himself on stage. *Beale St., Tel. 901/527-54 64*

Orpheum Theatre

Broadway shows, opera, light opera, film classics in a superbly – well worth a visit just to look at it – restored theatre. *Main St./Beale St., Tel. 901/525-30 00*

NASHVILLE

(102/C3) Up in the mountains of Tennessee there is yet another music venue, and, like Memphis, it's a modern metropolis bisected by freeways. Self-styled the 'Athens of the South', Nashville boasts numerous Neo-Classical, Victorian Gothic and earlier buildings. More pertinently, this really is *Music City USA,* to country music fans at least. Moreover, the city is rapidly becoming America's new capital of cars. The service sector, represented by insurance companies, is also noticeably present here.

SIGHTS

Opryland U.S.A.

The Disney World of country music with a theme park, several stages, itinerant buskers, bands and clowns. *Show and opening hours vary widely, Opryland USA pass for 2 days incl. a riverboat trip on the General Jackson US $99.95, Opryland USA reservations and tickets, 2808 Opryland Dr., Nashville, TN 37214, Tel. 615/889-66 11*

Plantations and Blues in the Bayous

These routes are marked in green on the map on the inside front cover and in the Road Atlas beginning on page 100

① FROM ATLANTA TO WASHINGTON

 This route takes you from the Olympic metropolis through the Appalachians to the capital of the United States. You'll drive most of the way north along the Atlantic seaboard, passing through colonial towns as well as the biggest cities in the South. The trip takes a week.

A modern metropolis *Atlanta (p. 46)* has little of the romantic charm of the Old South. If you want to drive right on, you leave the airport on I 85, heading north. At *Buford* you turn off on to US 23 and head for *Gainesville*. On US 441 you'll reach the mountains very quickly. This is the Appalachian system which extends from Georgia to Canada. The *Great Smoky Mountains (p. 84)*, which you reach via *Cherokee (p. 85; on US 74 veering slightly south and then to the right)*, are the most scenic and interesting part of the Appalachians. What is really lovely is the autumn *foliage*, when the trees turn red and gold. In the southern region of the Appalachians the leaves change quite a bit later(mid-October)than they do at the northern end of this vast mountain system.

You can drive north along the mountain ridges. The scenic routes you'll be taking to do this are the *Blue Ridge Parkway* and the *Skyline Drive (p. 43)*, which ends near Washington at *Front Royal (p. 43)* in Virginia. There are camping sites, log cabins and mountain lodges all along the route. Sometimes you'll look west; at others you'll see far to the east, where the mountains drop sheer to the fertile tobacco-growing Piedmont region in North Carolina and Virginia. Taking a day or two or even a few hours to hike along the *Appalachian Trail (p. 43)* is rewarding.

Once you're down in the plains you'll make up for lost time: on I 85 and – just before *Richmond (p. 42)* – on I 95. There are any number of towns along the way where you might want to stop and linger. In the mountains there's *Asheville*, a resort bisected by the rivers French Broad and Swannanoa. In the plains is *Winston-Salem*, a classic tobacco city with red brick processing plants and signs which nowadays are highly unusual, if not unique, in the health-conscious US: *We thank you for smoking.*

It's also interesting to drive westward on country roads. That way you'll see some of the poorer areas of Tennessee and West Virginia, where many people still work as hired hands in the region's scrubby fields or down in the coal mines.

One thing you definitely should do is take I 64 east to *Charlottesville (p. 35)* to visit the city with the most beautiful university campus in the US: the fabulous *University of Virginia* and *Monticello,* Thomas Jefferson's estate with the idiosyncratic house he designed. After staying the night near there, you can go on the next day along US 29 and US 211 to *Washington,* which any visitor to the US should take some time to see. There you'll admire the government buildings and museums along the *Mall.* When you've seen the elegant older residential part of the city, *Georgetown* and *Northwest (Connecticut and Nebraska Avs.),* you'll see why the nation's capital is called a sleepy Southern town.

Back in Virginia again, you must go to *Alexandria (p. 32).* The old part of town has hardly changed in the past two centuries. Then highway I 95 and I 64 take you south or southeast in two or three hours to the historical theme park and living museum at *Colonial Williamsburg (p. 39).*

At *Nagis Head,* North Carolina, you can go to the *Outer Banks (p. 40),* with huge sand dunes and deserted beaches. Via *Cape Hatteras (p. 40)* and *Ocracoke (p. 40)* ferries take you south again. You can book ferry space (signs along the road) or simply trust your luck. Ferries are only packed at summer weekends and especially on Memorial Day and Labor Day. Keep tuned into the weather report during the hurricane season (Jun–Sep)! Ferries don't run and island residents may even have to be evacuated: no fun at all!

US 17 takes you south to *Myrtle Beach,* a seaside resort clogged with kitsch which is not really recommended. You'd be far better off driving on and spending some time soaking up the ambience of the Old South in the lovely cities of *Charleston (p. 33)* and further down in *Savannah (p. 61).*

On your way back to Atlanta, you might want to make a detour to *Athens,* Georgia, especially if you happen to be fans of R.E.M., who live in this pretty town.

② FROM NEW ORLEANS TO MEMPHIS

 This route takes you to the mighty Mississippi, once the literary haunt of Tom Sawyer and Huckleberry Finn. Then on into the *Deep South,* and back again to the Gulf of Mexico. Time needed: a week.

You start off from *New Orleans (p. 75),* which is an absolute must. Then you might want to explore the *bayous,* Cajun country, the swamps and alluvial plains of the Mississippi Delta. To do so, you drive south from New Orleans on narrow country roads – the back country is fascinating. The Mississippi is a commercial waterway and the Delta is full of oil refineries and huge tankers and barges, which certainly aren't the paddle-wheel steamers Mark Twain spent so much time on in his youth. Near New Orleans is the town of *Jean Lafitte (State Roads SR 45 and SR 301),* where you can

90

take trips through the bayous on shrimp boats (like the ones in 'Forrest Gump').

You'll move faster on I 10 to *Baton Rouge (p. 74)* – the capital of Louisiana with Huey Long's weird-looking Capitol built of 26 kinds of marble. This is the end of the *Petrochemical Gold Coast,* an industrial belt which stretches 160 km from New Orleans to Baton Rouge, the state's second largest port. The *Sugar Bowl of America* starts here with vast sugar-cane plantations beyond the Mississippi.

Either you follow the river on SR 15 or drive directly on US 61 to *Natchez (p. 69),* with its superb *antebellum houses* (pre-Civil War). They are the subject of what is aptly styled *architecture pilgrimages. (Information obtainable from Natchez Convention and Visitors Bureau, Tel. 800/996-2824).* You then drive northeast on the *Natchez Trace Parkway (p. 71),* the route Indians, traders and settlers took *(roadside exhibitions and picnic grounds),* to *Jackson,* the capital of Mississippi.

From Jackson you head for Memphis on I 55. Devotees of best selling author John Grisham turn on to SR 6 for *Batesville* if the prospect of Faulkner's native postage stamp of soil at Oxford seems too depressing. *Memphis (p. 87),* the music metropolis on the Mississippi, where Elvis got his chance, is unabashedly modern but a good place to spend a night (the best place to stay is the grand old *Peabody Hotel)* right at the centre of town where the music is.

From Memphis you'll be driving through the back country of northern Mississippi and Alabama on US 78 to *Birmingham (p. 67),* once famous for steel but notorious in the 1960s when city

officials tried to sue *The New York Times* for libel when it reported racial injustice there. It, too, represents the New South without visible race problems and full of smokeless service-sector growth industries like insurance companies and health care. From there you take I 20 via *Tuscaloosa,* with fine pre-war houses in the Druid City District around Queen City Avenue, to US 43 and stay on to the port city of *Mobile,* which has an old section.

I 10 will take you back to New Orleans in no time. If you want a more leisurely trip, take US 90 via *Pascagoula, Biloxi (p. 66)* and *Gulfport.* The beaches along the Gulf of Mexico are usually flat and sandy and the water is warm for swimming from spring to autumn. A good many visitors are attracted to the area by the casino hotels which have mushroomed along this strip of coast.

③ FROM MIAMI TO TALLAHASSEE

 This route goes through Florida and part of it through southern Georgia, where there's still something left of 'Gone with the Wind'. Remember that in northern and central Florida the weather can be quite chilly from December to April. Time needed: a week; if you want to go down to Key West, allow for at least two more days.

In *Miami Beach (p. 55)* you should be up and off early in the morning when the sun is just going up in glorious Technicolor over the Atlantic. That way it'll still be early when you reach the *Everglades (p. 58; US 1 or the Florida Turnpike; the Turnpike toll is worth*

the much quicker trip), which is a unique wetlands region. If you're planning to go on to Key West at the very tip of the US, go on to US 1 near Florida city, where it becomes the *Overseas Highway,* and keep driving south, flying on over bridge after bridge across the glittering sea. Try to arrive at *Key West (p. 53)* just at sunset. You'll want to celebrate it with refreshing libations just as residents of this beautiful Key do.

The only way back to mainland Florida is the Overseas Highway. If you want to go to Sanibel Island, go right on to the Turnpike when you reach the mainland, then turn off on to I 75 – *Alligator Alley* – and head for Naples. Along this highway as well as on US 41 you really will see thousands of alligators enjoying the Florida sun on some days. However, if you do decide on the highways, you're in for traffic jams the whole way – the traffic is terrible in southern Florida. The multimillionaires on *Sanibel* and *Captiva* don't like seeing tourists in front of their sea-front mansions and try to deter them with high tolls and tickets for parking space. You can console yourself on the lovely beaches of *Naples, Ft. Myers Beach, Sarasota, St. Petersburg* and *Clearwater.* Unlike the Atlantic coast, which is cooled by trade winds in summer, the Gulf coast is unbearably hot and muggy then. There's almost no surf here and the silky soft sand is fine and white, shot through – on Sanibel especially – with shells.

The beaches on the Florida *Panhandle* are just as beautiful and it stretches far to the west along the Gulf. Between *Apalachicola* and *Pensacola* you'll find fabulous places for swimming but, unfortunately, some have been so spoilt by chains of cheap hotels that you might consider giving them a miss and driving straight on to the attractive state capital of *Tallahassee (p. 46).* via US 19 Just north of it and still within the Tallahassee conurbation begins southern Georgia at *Thomasville* and *Valdosta.* Here you'll find the Old South, with columned porches and – rather dilapidated – antebellum charm.

Back in Florida, you take the interstate highway I 75, I 10 and I 95 to *St. Augustine (p. 60),* the oldest or second oldest city in the US, depending on the dating criteria used. At *Daytona Beach (p. 50),* an hour's drive to the south, you simply must drive down that firm sandy beach. There's always a party going on here. Either students are enjoying a spring break or Harley-Davidson fans are roaring in for *Biker Week* early in March, not to mention the numerous car races at the Daytona Speedway.

Orlando (p. 58), the city of Disney World, Universal Studios and around a dozen other theme parks, offers round-the-clock entertainment. Just to the east of this fantasy world is the *John F. Kennedy Space Center (p. 59).* From here it's advisable to drive right to the Atlantic coast and take the A1A, which runs from *Cocoa Beach* for quite a while along the water. At *Palm Beach (p. 53)* you can have another good look at the very rich. *Fort Lauderdale (p. 51),* the last large town before you reach Miami, is growing into a viable alternative to Miami Beach, which has become too dangerous and too touristy for some.

Practical information

*Here you'll find the most important addresses
and brief information you'll need for your trip
through the Southern States*

AMERICAN & BRITISH ENGLISH

Marco Polo travel guides are written in British English. In North America, certain terms and usages deviate from British usage. Some of the more frequently encountered examples are:
baggage for luggage, billion for milliard, cab for taxi, car rental for car hire, drugstore for chemist's, fall for autumn, first floor for groundfloor, freeway/highway for motorway, gas (oline) for petrol, railroad for railway, restroom for toilet/lavatory, streetcar for tram, subway for underground/tube, toll-free numbers for freephone numbers, trailer for caravan, trunk for boot, vacation for holiday, wait staff for waiting staff (in restaurants etc.), zip code for postal code.

CAMPING

The most scenic camping sites are the public ones. They are usually located on lakes or in National Parks and are equipped with fireplaces, wooden picnic tables and benches and bathroom facilities. An overnight stay costs between US $5 and US $15. Private, often quite luxurious camping sites with hot showers, pools and shops can be found on the outskirts of cities and towns and in parks (prices approx. US $10–$30). Although camping anywhere you want is not expressly prohibited (except in parks), it is definitely frowned on in densely populated areas. If you plan to camp in a trailer (caravan), you should book it several months in advance. Bookings for sites in National Parks: *Tel. 800/365-22 67 (up to three months in advance).*

CUSTOMS

Objects for personal use are duty free. No plants, meats or other fresh foods may be brought into the US.

Adults are permitted 200 cigarettes or 50 cigars (no Cuban brands) or 2 kg tobacco as well as 1 litre alcoholic beverages and presents worth up to US $100.

DOMESTIC FLIGHTS

All large US airlines give discounts for domestic flight bookings if they are far enough in advance (usually at least 14 days) and round-trip tickets (you can always let the return ticket expire if you change your itinerary).

DRIVING

Roads are classified according to a numbering system. There are special road signs for each of the following: country roads, State and US Highways as well as the big Interstate Highways. Front and back seat belts must be kept fastened at all times. The speed limit on country roads is 55 m/h (88 km/h), in towns and residential areas 35 m/h (50 km/h). Only Interstate Highways may have a speed limit of 65 or at most 70 m/h (105 or 113 km/h). The blood-alcohol level permitted is 0.0.

Traffic rules and regulations are much as they are in continental Europe, the UK (driving on the right, of course) and Canada. Differences are: At traffic lights you can turn right even when you have a red light (unless expressly prohibited). On Interstate and State Highways overtaking on the right is allowed. However, it is forbidden, even for oncoming traffic, to overtake a schoolbus when it has stopped to permit pupils to get on or off. There is a regulation for *3-way-* or *4-way-stops,* intersections with stop signs at which vehicles coming from all directions must stop. The vehicle which stopped first may start first. The US Automobile Club AAA also helps members of similar organisations from other countries, so keep your membership card with you.

EMBASSIES & CONSULATES

Canadian Embassy
501 Pennsylvania Ave. NW,
Washington, D.C.;
Tel. 202/682-1755

British Embassy
3100 Massachusetts Ave. NW,
Washington, D.C. 20008;
Tel. 202/462-1340

British Consulate
845 Third Avenue,
New York NY 10022;
Tel. 212/745-0200

EMERGENCIES

The emergency call number nearly everywhere is *911,* which is toll-free from all telephones. In rural areas coin-operated telephones often list special numbers for police, fire and ambulance. When in doubt, call Operator *(0).*

HEALTH

Health care is top-notch in the US, but very expensive. Therefore, you must buy a special insurance policy with inclusive coverage before leaving home. Prescriptions for medication will be filled at *pharmacies* and *drugstores,* which are often open round the clock.

INFORMATION

General information:
The *USTTA (United States Travel and Tourism Administration)* has offices located throughout the world, generally in American embassies and consulates. Great Britain *Tel. 0171/495-4466; Mon–Fri 10 am–4 pm.*

American Society of Travel Agents (ASTA)
Tel. 800/965-2782
(24-hour hotline, toll-free when calling within the US)

Alliance of Canadian Travel Association,
1729 Bank Street, Suite 201, Ottawa, Ontario K1V 7Z5, Canada; Tel. 613/521-0474

Association of British Travel Agents
55-57 Newman Street, London W1P 4AH, England; Tel. 0171/637-244

Travel and Tourism Offices
(all 1-800 telephone numbers are for dialling within the USA)

Florida	904/487-1462
Georgia	800/847-4842
Kentucky	800/225-8747
Mississippi	800/927-6378
North Carolina	800/847-4862
South Carolina	800/346-3634
Tennessee	800/836-6200

MEASURES & WEIGHTS

1 cm	0.39 inches
1 m	1.09 yards (3.28 feet)
1 km	0.62 miles
1 m²	1.20 sq. yards
1 ha	2.47 acres
1 km²	0.39 sq. miles
1 g	0.035 ounces
1 kg	2.21 pounds
1 British tonne	*1016 kg*
1 US ton	*907 kg*

1 litre is equivalent to 0.22 Imperial gallons and 0.26 US gallons

MONEY

Banks are usually open 10 am–3 pm (Fri till 5.30 pm). They cash travellers' cheques (issued in US $ only!), but only large banks in big cities exchange foreign currency. You can exchange foreign currency at international airports as well as in some large hotels in big cities but the rate you receive will be bad.

Therefore, travel with US $ only! It is advisable to divide up your travel finances as follows: take about US-$100 *in cash* with you, *travellers' cheques* in US $ for every-day expenses (they are accepted in big cities and many restaurants and you'll be given change in cash), one of the standard international *credit cards* like Visa or Mastercard for bigger outlays (necessary for car hire) and emergencies. Credit cards are accepted everywhere. *Eurocheques* are virtually unknown.

The currency used is the American dollar, the 'greenback' (= 100 Cents). Dollars are issued in the following denominations: *(bills)* 1, 2, 5, 10, 20, 50 and 100 dollars and coins *(small change)* 1 ¢ *(penny)*, 5 ¢ *(nickel)*, 10 ¢ *(dime)*, 25 ¢ *(quarter)* and 50 ¢ *(half dollar)*. Dollar notes (bills) are of uniform size, of the same greenish-grey colour and differ only slightly in what is printed on them!

PASSPORTS & VISAS

Canadian citizens need valid proof of identity. For longer stays, better take a passport. Canadians do not require a visa, even if their visit exceeds three months. British citizens staying less than 90 days also do not need a visa prior to entering the United States. However, non-US residents must fill out an entry form upon entry.

POST OFFICE & TELEPHONE

Post offices are open Mon–Fri from 9 am to 5 pm; in big cities also Sat 8.30 am to 12 noon. Airmail postage to the EU is 84 ¢, for postcards 50 ¢. It takes 4–6 days for a card to reach Europe from a big city and usually 3–4 days longer from rural areas.

All telephone numbers in the USA have seven digits. Long-distance calls include a three-digit prefix known as the *area code*. For local calls, simply dial the seven-digit number. For long distance calls, dial '1', the area code and then the number.

Local calls from a public telephone cost 25 to 35 ¢. A computerized operator will announce the charge after a long-distance number is dialed. Please note: hotels often add high service charges. You'll save money by using a credit card, by first dialling the toll-free number of the telephone company, such as AT&T: 1-800-CALL ATT.

For assistance when making a telephone call, just dial '0' for the operator, who can also connect collect calls.

The prefix when calling from the UK to the USA is 001. The prefix when calling from Canada or the USA to Great Britain is: 011-44. Another bit of useful information for non-North American travellers: the toll-free numbers with the prefix '800' or '888' can be used to book flights, hotel accommodation and rental cars.

RENTAL CARS/TRAILERS

You need your country's driving licence or an international one to rent a car. Car hire is generally inexpensive, particularly in Florida (from US $25 a day, US $120 a week). Mileage is nearly always included in the price *(unlimited mileage)*. For full insurance coverage *(loss/damage waiver)* you pay a surcharge of US $10–$13 a day. Minimum age for car rental: 21. There are small, local car hire firms in addition to the big companies like Budget, Hertz, Avis and National. It's advisable to check cars from the smaller firms carefully and have this confirmed in writing before signing the rental contract. It's usually cheaper and more reliable to book your car in advance and return it where you picked it up so you avoid return charges. If you plan to drive your rental car in more than one state, you must indicate on your form: *out of state use.*

TAXES

Most states levy a surcharge of 4 to 7 per cent on food and purchases. You won't notice the *sales tax* until your bill comes! Hotels often have an overnight surcharge of more than one per cent.

TIME ZONES

Eastern Time Zone (GMT–5 hours) and *Central Time Zone* (GMT–6 hours). Daylight saving time from the first Sunday in April until the last Sunday in October.

TIPPING

A service charge is not included in prices listed on restaurant menus. So you should leave about 15 per cent of the bill as a *tip* on the table.

WHEN TO GO

The climate in the Southern States is subtropical and in places tropical. That means very long, hot summers with extremely high humidity. You can expect weather like this from May to September. A beautiful time of year is autumn, especially if you're lucky enough to experience *Indian Summer,* when the foliage has changed colour but the days are still pleasantly warm. This can be October or even November in the South. Winter can bring snow, especially in the northern regions of the South and the Appalachians. It never snows in southern Georgia, along the Gulf coast and Florida, although temperatures can drop to freezing. When it rains in the South, it usually pours, particularly in autumn and early winter. Spring comes suddenly in March/April. Only in southern Florida can you be sure of consistently mild temperatures with very little rain during the winter months of December and January. Except for Florida, the South is at its best during spring, early summer and autumn.

YOUTH HOSTELS

American Youth Hostels (**AYH**) cost between US $3 and US $25 per night. You'll generally find one in many of the larger cities and in some of the National Parks. A listing of the youth hostels is available in bookstores or at any national association of youth hostels: *Hostelling International, Vol. 2.* Another inexpensive alternative for accommodation is the *YMCA* (for men) and the *YWCA* (for women), although not every facility provides overnight accommodation.

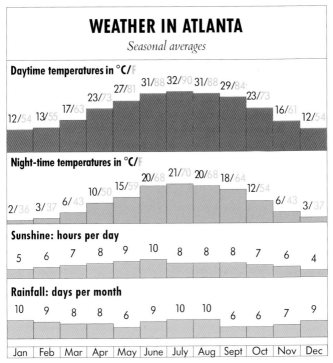

WEATHER IN ATLANTA
Seasonal averages

Daytime temperatures in °C/F

Jan	Feb	Mar	Apr	May	June	July	Aug	Sept	Oct	Nov	Dec
12/54	13/55	17/63	23/73	27/81	31/88	32/90	31/88	29/84	23/73	16/61	12/54

Night-time temperatures in °C/F

Jan	Feb	Mar	Apr	May	June	July	Aug	Sept	Oct	Nov	Dec
2/36	3/37	6/43	10/50	15/59	20/68	21/70	20/68	18/64	12/54	6/43	3/37

Sunshine: hours per day

Jan	Feb	Mar	Apr	May	June	July	Aug	Sept	Oct	Nov	Dec
5	6	7	8	9	10	8	8	8	7	6	4

Rainfall: days per month

Jan	Feb	Mar	Apr	May	June	July	Aug	Sept	Oct	Nov	Dec
10	9	8	8	6	9	10	10	6	6	7	9

Do's and don'ts

In the South – as everywhere else – pitfalls await the unwary visitor. Here are a few points to keep in mind

Air-conditioning

Cool Air systems – if you think you can't stand the chill in your B & B after the oppressive heat outside, you can ask your host or hostess whether the air-conditioning can be switched off in your room. Usually it can't. The entire house is on one system. Too bad, you'll miss the shrill and throbbing orchestra of insects and tree toads in the Southern night.

Politics and religion

Don't discuss them. School books mentioning evolution must print the following in Alabama: *This textbook discusses evolution, a controversial theory some scientists present as a scientific explanation for the origin of living things, such as plants, animals and humans. No one was present when life first appeared on Earth. Therefore, any statement about life's origins should be considered theory, not fact.*

Smoking

The anti-tobacco campaign is in full swing throughout the US even though the states of Virginia and North Carolina depend on tobacco for revenue and jobs. Smoking is forbidden on all domestic flights. In some places cigarette advertising is prohibited. Many restaurants and even bars have smoking zones. Hotels have smoking and non-smoking rooms and floors. If you're staying at a B & B in an old house, you'll find that smoking isn't even encouraged on the porch. So many of those 18th- and 19th-century houses are wooden and many are filled with English and American antiques.

Don't try to be a hero

Get those hands up! If you're attacked in the street, don't offer any resistance. Your attacker will be armed. Fork out any spare cash you have on you. The logical conclusion is, don't carry much cash around with you and don't flaunt it anywhere. Avoid all parks after sunset. This warning goes even during the day for those fantastic New Orleans graveyards which intrigued Mark Twain and, in recent years, have featured in Anne Rice's work. As in all US big cities, the crime rate is high in Atlanta, New Orleans and Miami. Avoid slums, where poverty and aggression go hand in hand. And in rural areas, never stop and knock on a door for help. Just hope you don't have a puncture on any of those bumpy roads. Guns in the family gun closet aren't just for squirrel hunting. The NRA (National Rifle Association) keeps its members close and loyal in the rural South.

Road Atlas of the Southern States

*Please refer to back cover for an overview
of this Road Atlas*

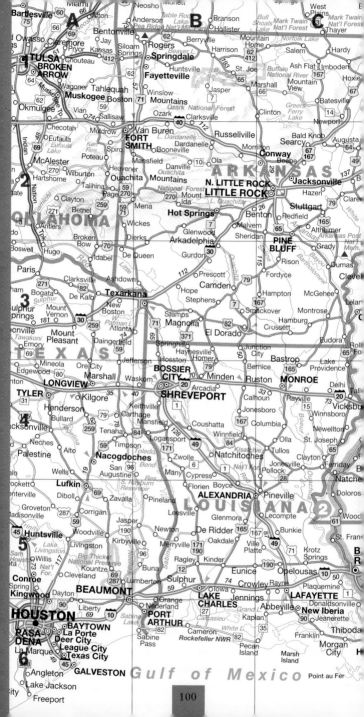

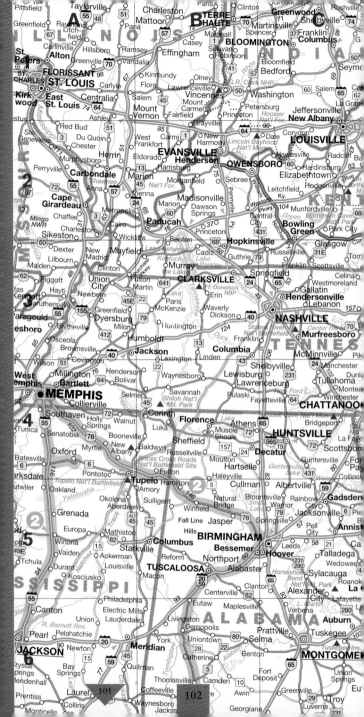

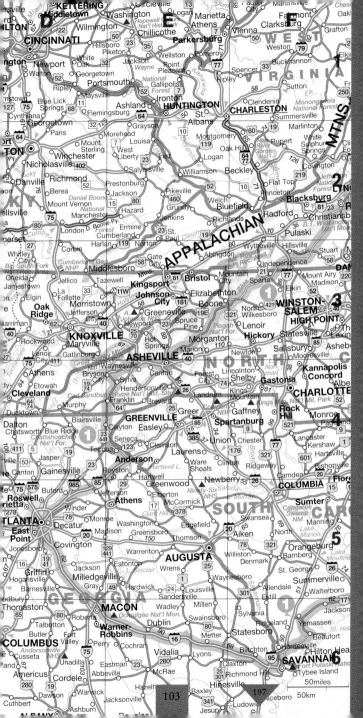

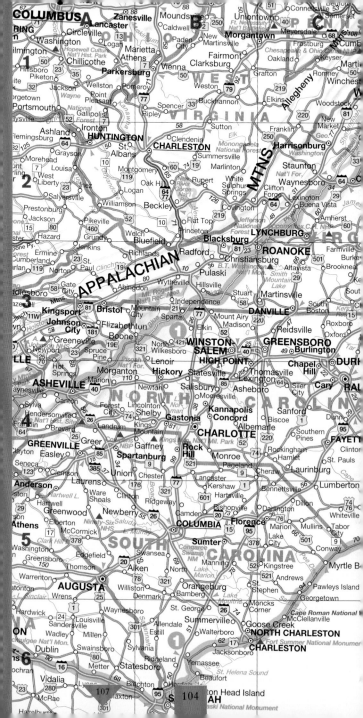

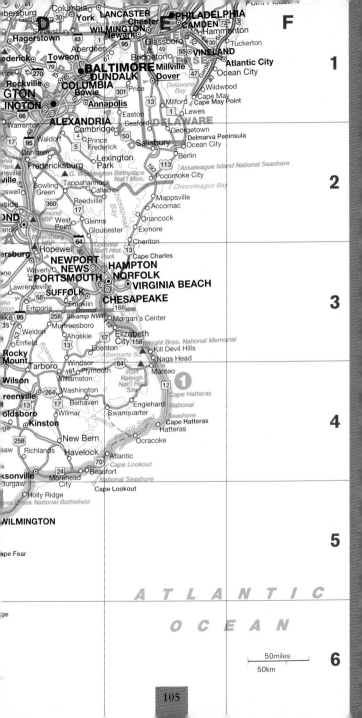

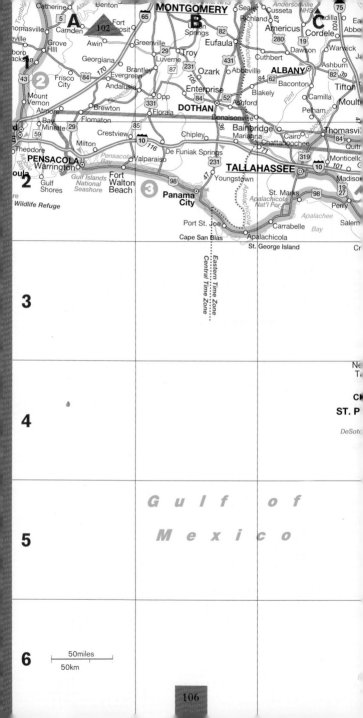

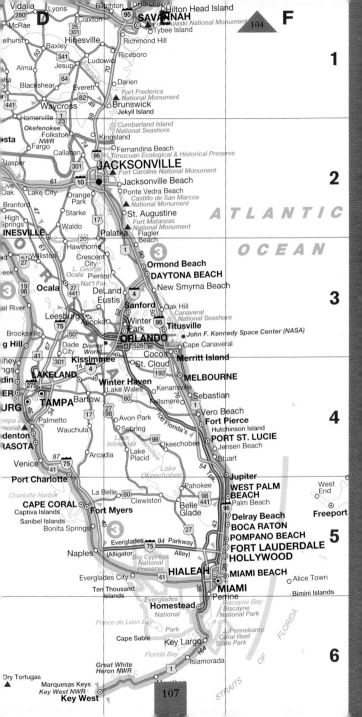

D

Vidalia
Lyons
Blitchton
Onarecheege
Hilton Head Island
95
SAVANNAH
McRae
Claxton
Tybee Island
elhurst
Hinesville
Richmond Hill
Fort Pulaski National Monument
104
F

Baxley
341
Ludowici
Riceboro
Jesup
Alma
Blackshear
84
Darien
1
ha
Waycross
Everett
82
Fort Frederica
49
National Monument
441
Homerville
23
Brunswick
Jekyll Island
sta
Okefenokee
Fargo
NWR
Folkston
Cumberland Island
National Seashore
Jasper
Callahan
Kingsland
301
Fernandina Beach
95
Timucuan Ecological & Historical Preserve
Live
JACKSONVILLE
Oak
10
Fort Caroline National Monument
Lake City
Orange
Jacksonville Beach
Branford
Park
Ponte Vedra Beach
61
High
Starke
St. Augustine
A T L A N T I C
Springs
17
Fort Matanzas
INESVILLE
Waldo
National Monument
Palatka
Flagler
Beach
O C E A N
ALT
Hawthorne
27
Crescent
1
Willston
City
3
L. George
Ocala
Pierson
Ormond Beach
19
Nat'l For.
DAYTONA BEACH
98
Ocala
27
New Smyrna Beach
3
441
DeLand
al River
Leesburg
Eustis
4
Sanford
Oak Hill
Apopka
Canaveral
75
National Seashore
Brooksville
50
Winter
95
Titusville
g Hill
Dade
Park
John F. Kennedy Space Center (NASA)
41
City
Disney
ORLANDO
301
World
528 36
Cape Canaveral
hey
Kissimmee
Cocoa
ngs
74
St. Cloud
Merritt Island
din
4
192
LAKELAND
Winter Haven
MELBOURNE
275
Lake Wales
Kenansville
TAMPA
Bartow
60
Sebastian
17
Fellsmere
ER
98
URG
27
Avon Park
Vero Beach
mpa Ba
Palmetto
Sebring
Fort Pierce
emorial
Wauchula
98
Hutchinson Island
Lake
PORT ST. LUCIE
denton
Okeechobee
Jensen Beach
RASOTA
Arcadia
Lake
Stuart
87
Placid
54 Tpk.
Venice
75
Lake
41
Okeechobee
Jupiter
Port Charlotte
Pahokee
West
Charlotte Harbor
La Belle
WEST PALM
End
CAPE CORAL
80
BEACH
Captiva Islands
Clewiston
Belle
98
Palm Beach
Freeport
Sanibel Islands
Fort Myers
441
Glade
Delray Beach
Bonita Springs
27
43
BOCA RATON
3
POMPANO BEACH
Everglades
75
94 Parkway
FORT LAUDERDALE
Naples
(Alligator
Alley)
Big Cypress
HOLLYWOOD
National
HIALEAH
MIAMI BEACH
Preserve
41
MIAMI
Alice Town
Everglades City
38
Perrine
Bimini Islands
Ten Thousand
Homestead
Biscayne Bay
Islands
Everglades
Biscayne
National
National Park
Ponce de Leon Bay
Pennekamp
Park
Coral Reef
State Park
Cape Sable
Key Largo
Florida Bay
164
Islamorada
6
Dry Tortugas
Great White
Heron NWR
Marquesas Keys
1
Key West NWR
STRAITS
107
Key West

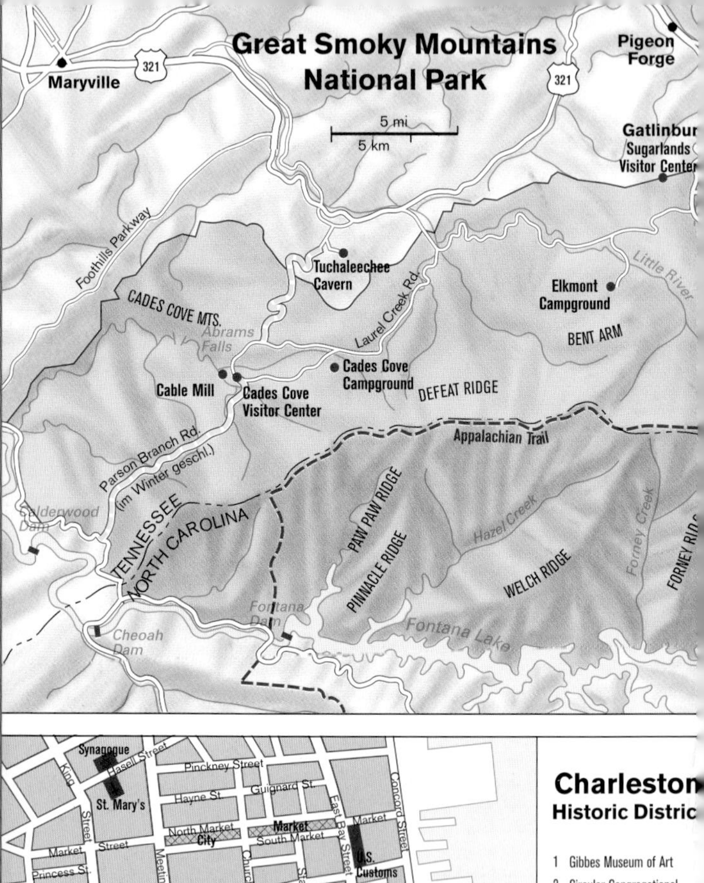
Great Smoky Mountains National Park
Maryville
321
Pigeon Forge
321
5 mi
5 km
Gatlinbur
Sugarlands Visitor Center
Foothills Parkway
Tuchaleechee Cavern
Little River
Elkmont Campground
CADES COVE MTS.
Abrams Falls
Laurel Creek Rd.
BENT ARM
Cades Cove Campground
Cable Mill
Cades Cove Visitor Center
DEFEAT RIDGE
Appalachian Trail
Parson Branch Rd. (im Winter geschl.)
Calderwood Dam
TENNESSEE
NORTH CAROLINA
PAW PAW RIDGE
PINNACLE RIDGE
Hazel Creek
Forney Creek
WELCH RIDGE
FORNEY RID
Fontana Dam
Cheoah Dam
Fontana Lake

Charleston Historic Distric

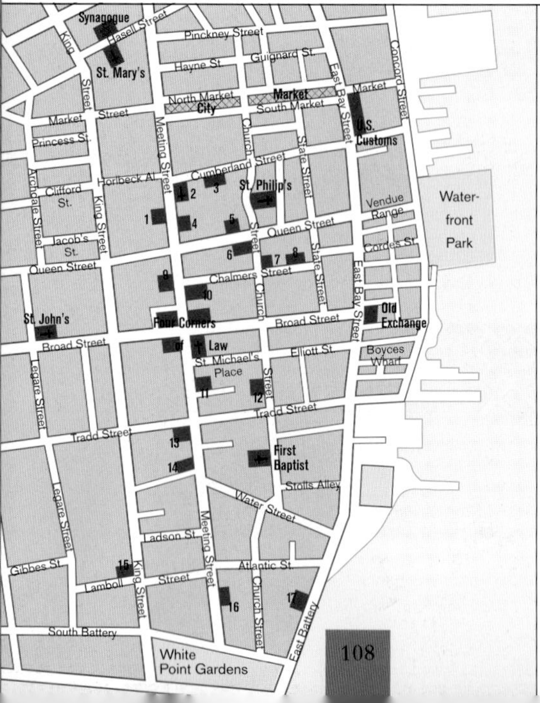
Synagogue
Hasell Street
Pinckney Street
Guignard St.
Hayne St.
St. Mary's
King Street
Concord Street
North Market
City
Market
South Market
Market
East Bay Street
U.S. Customs
Market Street
Princess St.
Meeting Street
Church Street
State Street
Cumberland Street
St. Philip's
Horlbeck Al.
Clifford St.
Archdale St.
Vendue Range
Water-front Park
Jacob's St.
Queen Street
Cordes St.
Queen Street
Chalmers Street
Old Exchange
St. John's
Four Corners of Law
Broad Street
Broad Street
Elliott St.
Boyces Wharf
St. Michael's Place
Legare Street
Tradd Street
Tradd Street
First Baptist
Stolls Alley
Water Street
Ladson St.
Gibbes St.
Lamboll Street
Atlantic St.
South Battery
East Battery
White Point Gardens

1 Gibbes Museum of Art
2 Circular Congregational Church
3 Old Powder Magazine
4 134 Meeting Street
5 Thomas Elfe Workshop
6 Dock Street Theatre
7 French Huguenot Church
8 Old Slave Mart
9 Hibernian Hall
10 Fireproof Building
11 S.C. Society Hall
12 Heyward-Washington House
13 First (Scots) Presbyterian Church
14 Nathaniel Russell House
15 Mile Brewton House
16 Calhoun Mansion
17 Edmonston-Alston House

0,2 mi
200 m

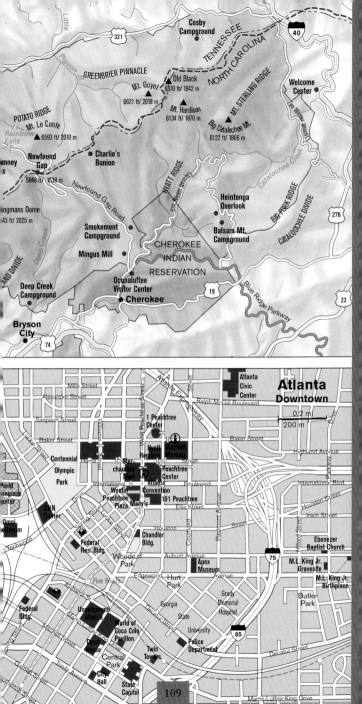

ROAD ATLAS LEGEND

German	Symbol	English
Gebührenfreie Autobahn	═══════	Controlled access highway
Gebührenpflichtige Autobahn	━━━━━━━	Controlled access toll highway
Hauptverbindungsstraße	━━━━━━━	Principal through highway
Nebenstraße	─────────	Other through highway
Interstate Highway	(20)	Interstate highway
US-Highway	98 68	US highway
Trans-Kanada-Highway / Mexican Federal Highway	✪ (14)	Trans-Canada highway / Mexican Federal highway
Bundesstaat-oder Provinzhighway	40 75	State or provincial highway
Entfernung (Meilen/Kilometer)	25 40	Distance (Miles/Kilometres)
Internationale Grenze	━━━━━━━	International boundary
Provinz- oder Bundesstaatengrenze	━━━━━━━	Provincial, territorial or state boundary
Fähre	– – – – –	Ferry
Zeitzonengrenze	··················	Time zone boundary
National-, Bundesstaat-, Provinzpark	━━━━━━━	National/state/provincial Park
Erholungs- oder Schutzgebiet	━━━━━━━	Recreational area or reserve
Natursehenswürdigkeit	▲	Natural point of interest
Kulturelle Sehenswürdigkeit	▲	Cultural point of interest

Einwohnerzahl:		Population:
Harrison	○	unter/less than 10 000
Camden	○	10 000 - 25 000
Muskegon	⊙	25 000 - 50 000
LONGVIEW	⊙	50 000 - 100 000
ALLENTOWN	◎	100 000 - 200 000
LONG BEACH	◉	200 000 - 500 000
MILWAUKEE	●	500 000 - 1 000 000
NEW YORK	●	über/more than 1 000 000
WASHINGTON		Hauptstadt / National capital
RICHMOND		Bundesstaats-/Provinzhauptstadt / State/provincial/territorial capital
Stadtgebiet		Built-up area

INDEX

This index lists all the main places and sights mentioned in this guide. Page numbers in bold typeface indicate main entries; page numbers in italics refer to photos

What do you get for your money?

The Southern States of the US are certainly not cheap, but for visitors from Europe, the dollar exchange rate is favourable. Extremely low flight prices are another advantage of travelling to the USA.

Prices in the US are determined by domestic factors and vary from place to place. The dollar seems to be doing pretty well on the currency market against both the Euro and the GBP, but rates fluctate constantly. Now for a basic sampling of US prices. A ticket on urban public transport costs about US $1. For the first mile a taxi driver charges approx US $3, and for each mile after that US $1.50. You rarely find a cup of coffee for less than US $1.50 yet a simple sandwich or hot dog needn't set you back more than US $2.50. Drinks start at US $3.50. Eating in restaurants is relatively inexpensive. In unpretentious eateries you can eat your fill for as little as US $10. Chain restaurants tend to be especially cheap. At these a meal costs US $5–$10. Motel rooms, comfortably furnished and with TV, can cost as little as US $30–$50. The price is for the room, not per person. You'll be lost without a credit card if you want to rent a car. Change is rarely given for notes (bills) of denominations above US $20.

US $	UK £	Can$
1	0.62	1.49
2	1.25	2.98
3	1.87	4.47
4	2.49	5.96
5	3.12	7.45
10	6.23	14.91
20	12.46	29.82
30	18.69	44.72
40	24.93	59.63
50	31.16	74.54
60	37.39	89.45
70	43.62	104.36
80	49.85	119.26
90	56.08	134.17
100	62.31	149.08
200	124.63	298.16
300	185.90	446.76
400	247.87	595.68
500	311.57	745.40
750	467.35	1,118.10
1,000	623.13	1,490.80